Talbot W. Chambers

**The Psalter**

a Witness to the Divine Origin of the Bible

Talbot W. Chambers

**The Psalter**
*a Witness to the Divine Origin of the Bible*

ISBN/EAN: 9783337100230

Printed in Europe, USA, Canada, Australia, Japan

Cover: Foto ©Lupo / pixelio.de

More available books at **www.hansebooks.com**

# A WITNESS

### TO THE

## *DIVINE ORIGIN OF THE BIBLE.*

BY

TALBOT W. CHAMBERS, D.D.,

ONE OF THE PASTORS OF THE COLLEGIATE DUTCH CHURCH OF NEW YORK.

NEW YORK:
ANSON D. F. RANDOLPH & COMPANY,
900 BROADWAY, COR. 20th ST.
1876.

Copyright, 1876, by
Anson D. F. Randolph & Company.

ROBERT RUTTER,
BINDER,
84 BEEKMAN STREET, N. Y.

EDWARD O. JENKINS,
PRINTER AND STEREOTYPER,
20 NORTH WILLIAM ST., N. Y.

# PREFACE.

This volume consists of a course of lectures delivered before the Theological Seminary and Rutgers College, New Brunswick, N. J., in the months of April and May last. The General Synod of the Reformed Dutch Church having seen fit to appoint the author to be Lecturer, on the Vedder Foundation, at a time when he was out of the country, and had neither expressed nor felt any wish on the subject, he felt constrained to accept the position, notwithstanding the fact that the pecuniary support of the Foundation had totally failed. The general subject of the lectureship is stated by the founder to be, "The present aspects of Modern Infidelity, including its cause and cure." The best "cure" of Infidelity is the study of the sacred volume which it rejects. With a view to promote this, the author selected a theme in the line of his recent studies, and treated it to the best of his ability. He is not aware that the argument here set forth has ever been handled in any separate volume. If, as thus presented, it shall satisfy any wavering minds, or if it shall prompt abler writers to a fuller and more convincing discussion of its varied aspects, he will be abundantly content.

NEW YORK, *September*, 1876.

# CONTENTS.

### LECTURE I.
INTRODUCTORY: THE NATURE OF THE PSALTER. . . . 1

### LECTURE II.
THE DOCTRINE OF GOD IN THE PSALTER. . . . . 37

### LECTURE III.
THE DOCTRINE OF MAN IN THE PSALTER. . . . . 73

### LECTURE IV.
THE MESSIAH AND THE FUTURE LIFE. . . . . . 113

### LECTURE V.
THE ETHICS OF THE PSALTER. . . . . . . 149

# LECTURE I.

INTRODUCTORY. THE NATURE AND CHARACTERISTICS OF THE PSALTER.

# LECTURE I.

## INTRODUCTION.

FORMS OF MODERN INFIDELITY — AGREE IN REJECTING THE SCRIPTURES—NEGATIVE AND POSITIVE METHODS OF DEFENCE—LATTER PREFERRED—THE PROPOSITION STATED—THE PSALTER CHOSEN BECAUSE IT BELONGS TO THE OLD TESTAMENT—BECAUSE SPONTANEOUS—BECAUSE SPIRITUAL—NATURE OF THE BOOK—ITS CONTENTS—AUTHORS—DATES—CLASSIFICATION—THE FIVE BOOKS—MOURNFUL—JOYFUL—DIDACTIC—GENERAL CHARACTERISTICS—1. POETICAL—PECULIARITIES OF FORM—2. LYRICAL—3. PALESTINIAN—4. TRUE—104TH PSALM—18TH PSALM—THE ARGUMENT *a fortiori*.

THE forms of modern infidelity differ widely among themselves, sometimes assailing single characteristic features of revealed truth; at others laying the axe at the root of all supernatural religion. The hottest controversy of the last half century had respect to the person of our Lord. The answers to His own weighty and searching question, "What think ye of Christ?" have declared that He was an intentional deceiver, or a victim of His own self-deception and enthusiasm, or an invention of His disciples and biographers, or a final result of mythical traditions gradually taking shape in an unintelligent age—all these being simply so many different ways of rejecting His own statement that He is the Son of the living God, and the Saviour of the world. Another form of the prevalent skepticism of our day is found in what the apostle once spoke of as " the oppositions of science falsely so called." This is not content with attacking some one great truth or fact asserted in our holy religion, such as the fall of man, the unity of the race, the occurrence of the deluge, or the resurrection of the Lord Jesus Christ, but cuts away the ground from under supernaturalism by insisting upon an absolute and unvarying uniformity in the sequences of nature from the very beginning. This theory of the unchangeableness of natural laws rules out revelation entirely, and remands us back to our own discoveries in the search for moral and religious truth.

Both these forms of error—the denial of the Lord Jesus, and the denial of the possibility of divine intervention in the processes of nature—agree in rejecting the Scripture as unworthy of trust because it states what is not true. Hence the pivot of the whole argument lies in the question, Is there a revelation come from God? or in other words, Is the Bible such a revelation? For however loosely men may talk of the different Scriptures of the ancient races as alike in character and authority, no serious person will undertake to set up any other professedly holy or divine book in competition with the lively oracles of God. The Vedas of the Brahmans, the Tripitaka of the Buddhists, the Avestan of the Parsis, the Koran of the Mohammedans claim to be divine, and are so regarded by their respective followers. But who now thinks of admitting the claim? These writings are all truly remarkable. They contain many striking thoughts, brilliant pictures, and glorious visions. Detached statements are found here and there which challenge universal admiration. But they lack not only in part, but altogether, the distinctive evidence of a revelation. They offer no specifications of time and place and circumstances to which the ordinary historical tests can be applied. Their warmest advocates claim for them no external evidences whatever. And when subjectively considered, these writings as a whole are found to be peculiarly local and national, not even pretending to that universality of meaning and application which must belong to a communication by God to man.

If anywhere on earth there is an authentic message from heaven, it must be in the Old Testament and the New. The argument to show that it is there may be conducted in two ways. One, the negative, takes up in detail the various objections which have been urged, and shows their unsoundness. This method has been pursued from the beginning in every age of the Church, indeed so extensively as to have given its name to the whole department of Christian evidences, which is now commonly known as *Apologetics*. The successful prosecution of this work demands time and space largely. Take, for example, the difficulties based on the discoveries of physical science. Much patience and learning are required to follow scientists through their elaborate investigation and argumentation, and carefully discriminate fact from theory, separating what is proved from what is inferred or conjectured. And when this is successfully done, there is often needed a special training in the hearer or reader to fit him to see the point of the objection or the force of the reply. And, besides, when one class of difficulties has been removed, all the others resting upon different grounds still remain to be taken up in turn and disproved.

The other method, therefore, the positive, that which considers and sets forth the grounds upon which our faith in the Bible as the Word of God rests, is both more complete and more satisfactory. It is true that the lines of argument are many, for it could not be otherwise in a book which is so large and varied in its contents, its history, and its relations to men. But each line of argument, if satisfactorily maintained, is not only good for itself, but concludes in favor of the whole. For example, if the miraculous attestations are made out to be what they profess, and God has actually set His seal to the written word, then the Bible is true, and all the other evidences, such as those drawn from the fulfilment of prophecy, from the substance of the Bible, from its purity and harmony, its truth to human nature, its benign influence upon the individual, the family, and the State, the rapid propagation of its faith, and the like, are also true, and give the argument cumulative force. And so with any one of these compared with the rest. Truth is the same always and everywhere. A revelation which is true historically must be also true on all other grounds, theoretical or practical. Milton, in his *Liberty of Unlicensed Printing*, mentions the Egyptian fable that " Typhon with his conspirators took the virgin Truth, hewed her lovely form into a thousand pieces and scattered them to the four winds," from which time her sad friends have gone up and down in careful search, "gathering up limb by limb still as they could find them." But the dissevered pieces must needs make one whole, and each as it turned up was a pledge of the existence of the rest. And so each successful argument for the supreme truth interlocks with all the others and carries them along with it. As Hooker says, " Truth, of what kind soever, is by no kind of truth gainsaid."

If a choice is to be made among the various methods of sustaining the faith, I quite agree with the sentiment expressed in the previous course of lectures on this foundation by Dr. TAYLER LEWIS: "The Bible itself must be brought out as the best defence against infidelity—the Bible itself, not only as the great standing miracle of history, but as containing unearthly ideas for which no philosophy, no theory of development can ever account. . . . . Other defences are indeed important, but without this they are shorn of the great strength which can alone make them available to the pulling down of strongholds, and the overthrow of the truth's unwearied foes." A further reason for taking this course is found in the fact that the most interesting branch of Apologetics to ordinary readers, and especially to devout Christians, is that which treats of the Scripture's own claims for what it is, in and of itself. This is a portable manual of the evidences always at hand, and always available for an answer to them that ask a reason of the hope that is in us. But the whole Bible, or even one Testament, is far too large for a course of lectures like this. I have chosen, therefore, to take up a single book, one that is complete in itself, and yet stands in vital relation to all the rest, viz.: the Psalms. The proposition is that these Psalms as a whole, when viewed as to their subjects, aims, spirit, and teaching, especially in comparison with the corresponding literature of all other forms of religion, can be accounted for on no other ground than a divine origin.

This theme is selected because, first, it belongs to the Old Testament, which is always more sharply assailed than the New, and which, as the introductory portion of a gradual revelation, for that very reason stands the more open to hostile criticism. Hence it follows that if a constituent part of that which is professedly an incomplete and preparatory disclosure of the divine will can be substantiated on independent grounds, much more may that which belongs to the full and final statement of God's Word. The timidity of some Christian writers on this point is unaccountable. They seem to speak of the Hebrew Scriptures as if they were a burden to carry. How much nobler and truer is the language of the accomplished and genial critic, HERDER, in the preface to his *Geist der Ebräische Poesie:* "The basis of theology is the Bible, and that of the New Testament is the Old. It is impossible to understand the former aright without a previous understanding of the latter; for Christianity proceeded from Judaism, and the genius of the language is in both books the same. And this genius of the language we can nowhere study better—that is, with more truth, comprehensiveness, and satisfaction—than in its poetry, and, indeed, as far as possible, in its most ancient poetry. It produces a false impression and misleads the young theologian to commend to him the New Testament to the exclusion of the Old. Without this that can never be understood in a satisfactory manner. In the Old Testament we find as an aid to this a rich interchange of history, of figurative representation, of characters, and of scenery; and we see in it the many-colored dawn, the beautiful going forth of the sun in his milder radiance. In the New Testament it stands in the highest heavens and in meridian splendor, and every one knows which period of the day to the natural eye imparts most life and strength."\*

The spontaneous character of the Psalms gives a further reason for selecting them. They are thus sharply defined and discriminated from the most of the other writings with which they are connected. Every reader at once recognizes the difference between a chapter of moral or ceremonial precepts, or a historical narrative or a logical argument, and the outburst of passion or sentiment which gives character to a poetical utterance, especially when it takes the form of a lyric. In the latter there is a buoyancy of life, a freshness of feeling not seen elsewhere. The singer has his tongue unloosed

---

\* Marsh's Translation, I., 22.

from every bond, and under some overmastering impulse pours out what he sees and feels. He pursues no course of consecutive reasoning, draws no nice distinctions, elaborates no speculative theme, but simply utters, in such phrase as the place and the time suggest, that which deeply stirs his own heart. Consequently all is free, unstudied, natural. Even where the conceptions are most sublime, or the images most striking, or the words most felicitous, art lingers behind nature, and we feel ourselves in the presence of a soul moved to its depths. If, now, it can be shown that in such passionate utterances as these which arouse and express

> All thoughts, all passions, all delights,
> Whatever stirs this mortal frame,

that even amid the highest flights of imagination, and a very whirlwind of contending feelings, there is yet an element truly divine that dominates the whole and separates it by an impassable gulf from all other poetry, ancient or modern, the conclusion holds good not only for the Psalter, but for the entire volume of which it is an integral part.

Another attractive feature of the Psalms for the present purpose is their spiritual character.

They are wonderful not only for their antiquity, their variety, their simplicity, their frequent sublimity, pathos, tenderness, and fire, but also for a peculiar development of thought and feeling. They acquaint us with the interior life of the Old Testament saints; they disclose to us their feelings in the most sacred and hallowed moments of their lives; they give us a deep insight into the more hidden wonders of a holy religion, showing how our common humanity is affected under the experimental application of a true and self-consistent theology. Other parts of the Old Testament furnish the didactic statements of religious truth, its precepts or its promises, or its illustration in history or biography; but in the Psalter we come close to the beating heart of the believer; we see the actings of the whole moral nature in the presence of vivid, spiritual realities; we trace the working of faith, and hope, and gratitude, or of shame, and fear, and penitence; we follow the entire course of spiritual vicissitudes in the dealings of the individual soul with its Maker and Portion; in short, there is a perfect mirror of the devout man's inward life. Hence it is that so often the Psalms and the New Testament are bound up in the same volume, and lie on the table or the pillow of many an humble Christian for whom the poetic power, the lyric fire, the graceful allusions, and the vivid imagery have little or no charm, but who sees in the picture of soul conflicts, of lowly abasement, of penitential confession, of rapt adoration, of clinging faith and sacred joy, the very stimulus and comfort his own situation requires. Doctrine and duty are translated before his eyes into experience, and the transcript goes straight to his heart. Utterances made thousands of years ago in the Cave of Adullam or in the courts of the temple, are as fresh and life-like to his apprehension as if they originated but yesterday in his own land. If this be the fact—and how can it for an instant be doubted?—in dealing with the Psalter we are not at work upon the outposts, but in the citadel of Revelation, at close quarters with the very secret of its strength. Its acknowledged excellence in this respect, its fidelity to the intuitive instincts of enlightened souls, unmarred by the excesses of superstition or enthusiasm, require us to seek its origin higher than on the plane of this earth.

What, then, is the Psalter? In the form in which it stands in our Bibles—a form which can be conclusively traced back to the middle of the third century before Christ—it is a collection of one hundred and fifty lyrics, marked by very great differences among themselves, yet on the other hand united by certain features which they have in common. The differences are patent on even a superficial inspection. For example, in the matter of length they vary from one of two sentences (cxvii.) to one of a hundred and seventy-six (cxix.); and between these two extremes there is a constant diversity, denoting the absence of any prescribed pattern. The authors, too, are various. Although the book is commonly called the Psalms of David, yet he is the recognized author of only seventy-three, a little less than one-half of the whole. Still the title is justly given, since he was probably the composer of others, and the entire book evidently took its characteristic features and tone from him. More than fifty psalms are anonymous, while twelve are assigned to Asaph, eleven to the sons of Korah, two to Solomon, one to Ethan, and one to Moses, the man of God. The oldest known division of the collection is into Five Books, terminating respectively with Pss. xli., lxxii., lxxxix., cvi., and cl. These books are separated and distinguished from each other by the doxologies with which they severally conclude, by the greater or less use of one or other of the divine names, and by a general progress from doctrine and experience in the First, through historical and didactic utterances in the Second and Third, to a dominant tone of praise and triumph in the Fourth and Fifth. This ancient division suggests what on other grounds seems a rational hypothesis, that the collection as we have it is one that was gradually made through a long course of time — each book marking a new accretion to the original stock. For this reason it is not surprising to find the composition of some lyrics separated by a considerable interval from that of others. The oldest is the one (xc.) ascribed to Moses — an ascription which, although often and severely attacked, can yet be successfully vindicated. Others are by common consent attributed to the period of the Exile or the Restoration. Some writers have assigned certain Psalms to the Maccabees — a view in which Calvin so far shared as to consider that Pss. xliv., lx., lxxiv., and lxxix. were composed during the persecuting reign of Antiochus Epiphanes. But it is not necessary to defend at length the traditional view on this point, since even so independent a thinker as EWALD, whose scholarship and insight no one disputes, scouts the Maccabean authorship as destitute of any rational grounds.  Taking, then, the age of Malachi as the time when the collection was completed, we have a body of literature whose beginning is separated from its end by a thousand years—a space more than half as long again as that between Homer and Anacreon, or between Chaucer and Tennyson.

But great as is the diversity of authorship and date, equally great is that of tone and spirit. All are by no means pitched in the same key. Avoiding minute details, I may specify three general divisions as indicating the variety of feeling and utterance.  One is the Pathetic, or Mournful.  A tradition as old as Origen gives to seven (vi., xxxii., xxxvi., li., cii., cxxx., cxliii.) the title of Penitential Psalms, but these are far from exhausting the list of such as may fairly be thus described.  Indeed it is remarkable how amply the literature of sorrow is represented in this book.  No sufferer of any period, whether from age or infirmity, or bereavement, or desertion, or treachery, or persecution, or exile, or any form of spiritual perplexity or darkness, fails to find an appropriate expression of his feelings. So vivid are these utterances of the soul that no one can mistake them for flights of fancy. They are, they must be, the records of a real experience. In strong contrast with the "hearse-like airs," as Bacon calls them, are the Songs of Praise and Joy. The themes here are very various; a recent deliverance from danger, a victory over national foes, the downfall of a persecuting tyrant, the glory of God expressed in His works, the same glory shining out in providential interpositions, the perfections of the Most High, and especially the displays of His loving-kindness. Here, again, is a fitting vehicle for the expression of similar feelings in all ages and countries. Thanksgiving and praise on whatever ground have a pattern in these old Hebrew lyrics, which leaves nothing to be desired. But what is truly remarkable, a feature which occurs nowhere else that I know, sometimes both styles are united in the same composition. The writer begins in the deepest distress, a wail *de profundis*, but gradually, sometimes suddenly, passes into a strain exactly opposite; and the groans and complaints of the first part are drowned in the triumphant hallelujahs of the second (vi., xiii., xxxi., etc.) But besides these impassioned utterances, there is a class of didactic or even gnomic compositions which are scarcely less interesting or useful. These for the most part set forth the character of the good man and the bad, and the consequent happiness or misery of their respective conditions, or the varied excellencies of the divine law, or the vanity of human pursuits, or the duties of particular classes of men. Modern precision has objected to some of these as unsuited for lyrical purposes, but they were certainly sung or cantillated in the ancient Church, and the majority of the Christian Church in all ages, has found its account in cherishing didactic compositions as an integral part of the service of song in the house of the Lord.

But while the Psalms have the differences which have been mentioned, and bear such strong marks of individuality, there are several features which belong to them in common, and give to them a unity of character, which quite forbids the thought that they are scattered and random utterances accidentally or capriciously gathered into a book.

First, they are *poetical*, all of them. Of course not in the sense in which we apply that term to the verse of the ancient classics, or to that of any modern literature. The Hebrews knew nothing of rhythm or rhyme. A fearful amount of ingenuity and research has been wasted in vain endeavors to find some regular measures corresponding to the metres of the western nations. Nor does there seem any reason to suppose that the result would be different, did we know (as confessedly we do not) the exact method of the ancient pronunciation of the language. Metres have not been discovered because they did not exist. Did they exist, we may be sure that the penetration which has unlocked the secrets of Hieroglyphic, Cypriote, and Cuneiform inscriptions would long since have shown the fact to the satisfaction of all. As the case stands, there is no more measured verse in the Hebrew Psalter than there is in the authorized version of the same. And we may well rejoice that it is so. Were it otherwise, how greatly would the difficulties of translation into other tongues be multiplied! It is hard enough to convey the sense of one language justly and gracefully into another, but the task is far sorer when form as well as substance has to be reproduced. Any good Greek scholar can give the full and exact meaning of a ringing chorus of Æschylus or Sophocles, but not all combined can reproduce in English the music of the harmonious numbers employed by the original poet. Our literature abounds in imitations, but they *are* imitations, and as much like the original as a wax flower is to what it represents—as much, but no more. There may be the perfection of mechanism, but there is no life. On the contrary, the poetical form of the Psalms can be perfectly well represented in almost any language. There is a versified structure, but the versification does not depend upon sounds or words or accents, but upon things. Instead of being verbal, it is real. The relation between the successive lines of a Hebrew poem does not lie in the harmony of the words, but in the harmony of the ideas. Every poetical utterance of every kind, long or short, literal or figurative, animated or calm, is made up of a series of balanced sentences or propositions, each of which corresponds in some way to the rest. This feature, called Parallelism by Lowth, who, though he by no means was its discoverer, yet was its most skilful and successful expounder, is the key to the entire structure. One clause leads us always to expect another, which shall either repeat the sentiment of the first, or set forth its opposite, or give a variation of the theme. The Parallelisms have been classified and named by various writers, but minutiæ on this point are of no value. The one essential thing is that the poetical form lies in the relation of the clauses or sentences, and necessarily carries with it the thought. Hence the truth of the remark so often made as to its unchangeable character in all versions, however rudely made. As Bishop Jebb says, " Hebrew poetry is universal poetry, the poetry of all languages and of all peoples ; the collocation of words is primarily directed so as to secure the best possible announcement and discrimination of the sense. Let, then, only a translator be literal, and so far as the genius of the language will permit, let him observe the original order of the words, and he will infallibly put the reader in possession of all, or nearly all, that the Hebrew text can give to the best Hebrew scholar of the present day." Of course there are linguistic peculiarities which can not be reproduced in a modern tongue —such as the use of archaic terms, the introduction of peculiar grammatical forms and terminations, and, at times, the employment of words, which suggest at once to a vernacular reader what could not be conveyed to another except by a tedious periphrasis—as, for example, in Isaiah lx. 1, we read, "The glory of the Lord is risen upon thee." The version is faithful, yet it does not convey to the English reader what the original does to the Hebrew, viz., that this glory would rise upon Zion with the same majesty and beauty with which the sun rises over the earth. But apart from these exceptions, every literal version of Hebrew poetry in any tongue, gives to the reader a full and faithful impression of its beauty, sublimity, and force, whereas a bald prosaic rendering of the Iliad or of the Divina Commedia, would make one wonder where the far-famed glory of the original had gone.

(2). But the Psalms are not only Poetical, but also, as has been said, belong to that species of poetry which is called *Lyrical.* The Hebrews had no epic and no drama. The argument of Ewald (*Die Dichter des A. B.*, I. 69, seq.) to show the existence of a theatre in the days of David and Solomon, is a conspicuous failure, which not even his profound insight and vast learning could avoid. To call Job a tragedy and Canticles a comedy, simply shocks common sense. But the dramatic element, so far as concerns representation of character, and dialogue, and refrain, and chorus, is not wanting even in the shorter utterances of the Hebrew muse, because they are for the most part pure lyrics, unquestionably the oldest form of poetry and the fruitful germ of all others. It is as Ewald says, "The daughter of the moment, of swiftly rising, powerful feelings, of deep, stirring, and fiery emotions of the soul by which the poet is altogether carried away." It is a direct outpouring of the heart, the result of an impulse springing from the very foundations of our nature, to express in words what powerfully stirs within. But these words must in form correspond with that which they express, and hence they take the peculiar shape which we call poetic. The singer sings, in the first instance at least, to satisfy this inward pressure, and has no thought or aim beyond his immediate subject. Hence while his words take form, it is always form of the simplest kind, parallel utterances, strophes, refrains, occasional assonances, and the like, never rhymes or measured syllables. The development of the thought is varied by striking images of all kinds, by numerous personifications of inanimate nature, by the introduction of changing scenes and persons, unexpected applications, sharp transitions, and the boldest anthropomorphic representations of God and divine things. Yet all bears the unmistakable stamp of freshness and originality. Song never deals with the abstract, but with the concrete. It is personal and emotional. It starts from the feelings, and it speaks to the feelings. It is therefore intensely human. That element not only lies upon the surface, but pervades warp and woof of the whole. Hence always the lyrics of a people or a period are the truest expression of its character. When Lord Macaulay was seeking the materials for his incomparable history, he made diligent search for every popular ballad, for every dingy half-sheet, as that which gave the very form and spirit of the time. And he was right. Other forms of utterance may be borrowed or imitated, but song wells up from the heart, and indicates unerringly what it is that stirs the interior recesses of the soul. A genuine singer sings not because he wants to sing, but because he must. The passion swelling within demands expression and will not be denied.

(3). Accordingly the Psalter is eminently Hebraistic, or rather *Palestinian*, bearing in all its parts the evidence of its origin. None of its characteristic features came from without. Even cultivated Egypt, where the seed of Abraham accomplished the slow transition from a family to a nation, exerted no influence here. Learned men have often tried to deduce the Mosaic ritual and cultus from Egyptian memories and traditions, but so far as I know, only one (De Rongé, *Revue Contemporaine*, 1856,) has ever dreamed of tracing Hebrew poetry to the land of the Pharaohs. The very thought is absurd. How could that rainless region with its one river and its one monotonous plain from the cataracts to the sea, suggest the boundless and varied stock of images and expressions which are found in the Psalms? These in their combination could come alone from such a land as Palestine, with its hills and dales; its fountains, wells, and brooks; its lakes and seas; its deep gorges; its lofty precipices; its snows and hail, and ice, and storm, and whirlwind; its orchards and vines, and pastures, and grain fields, and gardens; its fragrant and gorgeous wild flowers; its dense forests, where birds sing among the branches, and wild beasts crouch in their dens; its continual outlook upon the great sea on one hand, and the great desert on the other. The Holy Land is as distinctly marked by its natural peculiarities as it is by its history and traditions. Its physical geography is unlike that of any other country on the face of the globe. No where is there such a furrow on the earth's surface as that made by the Jordan in its rapid and tortuous course from the roots of Hermon to the beautiful, yet awful gulf of Siddin. The summit of Lebanon is a little short of the limit of perpetual snow, while the Dead Sea is 1,300 feet below the ocean level; and therefore between these limits are found the temperatures of all zones and their productions; the palm and the sugar cane, and the cotton, and the fig, along with the apple, the wheat, the barley, and the grape. As Isaac Taylor says in a remarkable chapter of his *Spirit of the Hebrew Poetry* (London Ed., p. 72), "Palestine in the age of its wealth was a samplar of the world; it was a museum country—many lands in one; the tread of the camel in two or three hours, may now give the traveller a recollection of his own—come whence he may, from any country between the torrid zone and our northern latitudes. . . . . Thus it was that the Hebrew poet found always near at hand those materials of his art which the poets of other lands had to seek for in distant travel. Imagery, gay or grave, was around him everywhere, and these materials included contrasts the most extreme."

Yet while the tone and coloring are thus local, while the range of allusion and the wide diversity of natural symbols point unerringly to a Palestinian origin, the moulding and characteristic features come from the poet himself. His imagery bears the color and flavor of the soil, but he handles it for his own purposes. He possesses and is not possessed by his materials. Matter is constantly subordinated to spirit, and nature to God.

(4). Once more, the Psalter is absolutely *true*. This needs to be emphasized, because there are those who think that its poetical character is inconsistent with trustworthiness. A maxim in universal use treats truth and poetry as if they were irreconcilable opposites. And Goethe wrote an autobiography which he entitled "Poetry and Truth: from my own Life," in which the contrast is very evident. The proportions of reality and romance are like those of "the half pennyworth of bread and the intolerable deal of sack," in Falstaff's bills. Real incidents are poetically treated, *i. e.*, in such a way as to give a very different impression from that which an actual spectator of them would receive. It is quite otherwise with the Psalms. In them we have an exemplification of the statement that poetry is essential truth allied with feeling, with imagination, with appropriate and vigorous expression. It is truth not argued, inferred, or proved, but truth seen and felt—truth filling the soul and then pouring itself forth as a fountain bursts out of the earth. It is concerned, not with the accidental and temporary, but with the necessary and eternal, with the essence of things rather than details. Hence the profound Aristotle, himself anything but a poet, affirmed (*De Poet.* ix.) "that poetry is a more philosophical and a more serious thing than history itself." For history treats of τα καθ'εκαστον, what is individual, and may or may not be repeated, but poetry of τα καθ'ολον, what is universal, true in all places and for all time. Hence the poet, according to his name, is the maker. He does not copy, but creates. His work is the ideal embodied in and shining through the real. It gains at first hand, and as if by inspiration, what other writers and speakers reach by slow and tentative processes.

In consequence of the subjective nature of lyric poetry, and the intense mental action it implies, there is, one can not deny, a tendency to excess, to extravagance in thought and utterance. Yet those who are confessedly the greatest of epic poets—Homer, Dante, Milton—are marked by their truth and simplicity, by a calm repose, a sustained grandeur, resulting from conscious power. The same result is reached in the Psalter, but in another way. The flame of emotion glows through and through its utterances, transfiguring and ennobling everything, but it is always true to nature when nature is truest to virtue and to wisdom. The singer's object is not to win admiration by the splendor of genius, not to charm a listening multitude by tricks of invention or graces of song, but to please and honor the God of truth by articulating what He himself inspired, or by giving form and shape to the most real and living experiences of the human soul. Hence the absence of all that is unsuitable in theme or treatment. No erotic songs, no pæans to a national hero, no brilliant ideals of humanity, no meretricious ornament, nothing to dazzle, bewilder, or delude, nothing unreal or sophisticated, but everything stamped all the way through with the tokens of absolute truth. Take, for example, the One Hundred and Fourth Psalm, a divine ode of creation, a lyrical poem in which, as

Humboldt says, "we are astonished to find in such limited compass, the whole universe—the heavens and the earth sketched with a few bold touches. The contrast of the labor of man with the animal life of nature, and the image of omnipresent, invisible Power renewing the earth at will or sweeping it of its inhabitants, is a grand and solemn poetical creation." The sacred songster follows the first chapter of Genesis. What Moses represents in narrative prose, the psalmist sets forth in a series of living pictures, which, for depth of color, brightness, tenderness, beauty, and grace, have never been surpassed. It is a continuous series of vivid images—Jehovah clothed with light as a garment, making the clouds His chariot, and moving upon the wings of the wind; the wild ass quenching his thirst at streams which God provides; the birds singing among the branches; the wild goats finding a home in inaccessible crags; the young lions seeking from God their prey; the sea with the same fulness of life—its depths peopled with monsters, and its surface studded with sails; and then, in fine contrast with this animal activity of lower creatures, the even tenor and calm dignity of man's daily life of labor. Yet with all this exuberant energy and fertile play of the imagination, there is not a single false note, not a solitary departure from the purest and highest truth. On the contrary, even the early record in Genesis, so remarkable as to have attracted the praise of the heathen Longinus, does not set forth so strikingly the infinite greatness, the order, the life of the universe, and its absolute dependence upon God.

The same thing is vividly illustrated in another and very different psalm, the Eighteenth. This is a grateful retrospect by David of his peculiar career down to the time when he sat upon the throne of all Israel, and saw his enemies on all sides subdued. He begins with a series of lively figures denoting what God had been to him during his pilgrimage—his rock (of strength), his fortress, his deliverer, his rock (of refuge), his shield, his horn of salvation, his high tower. Then after setting forth the desperate extremities in which he had fallen, he describes his deliverance. But how? Not by a minute recital of his conflict with the lion and the bear, or with Goliath, his escape from the spear of Saul or the bows of the Philistines, his refuge at Adullam or Engedi, the defeat of the men of Keilah, or the means by which the hot pursuit of the fugitive was again and again checked just at the point of success. No; he masses all together, as if performed at one time and by one act, and pictures the whole as a magnificent Theophany. God comes to the rescue as He came of old to Sinai, and all nature is moved at His coming. The earth quakes and even mountains reel. Amid vaporous clouds the blaze of lightning is seen. Then the heavens seem to sink toward the earth, and amid the increasing gloom, behold, Jehovah riding upon the Cherubim, flying upon the wings of the wind. Darkness is His pavilion round about Him, but the brightness of His presence dissipates the gathering clouds and the full fury of the storm bursts forth. Thunder and lightning, hailstones and coals of fire, scatter all foes, and lay bare the depths of the sea and the very foundations of the world. The consequence is the swift and certain deliverance of David. Now not a word of this is to be taken literally. The whole is a grand poetic picture, transferring to an individual experience the memorable display at the giving of the law. At no time did David see, except in imagination, the burning coals, the flying Cherub, the bared sea-bottom. Yet he has truly expressed the fact in relation to the marvellous Providence which watched over his course from the sheepfold to the throne.  The actual care of God for His servant was as real and great, and effective as it could have been, had He came down in person to manifest it.  The lofty lyric is therefore true.  It is not mere poetic license or fancy's exaggeration, but the vivid lyric expression of what occurred, not once only, nor twice, but over and over during a lifetime.

Now it is just this truth of the Psalter which is the foundation of the argument I have undertaken to present.  That argument is strictly *a fortiori*.  Leaving out of view the prose of Scripture, its history, its dogma, its ethics, its prophecy, whatever belongs to the discursive faculty, and treating only of one of those portions in which imagination and feeling predominate, the aim is to show that here where exaggeration and error might most of all be looked for, where tongue and pen run riot, where it is common to excuse aberrations from propriety on the ground that the poet must needs have license, just here there is no need for any abatement or qualification whatever. Wide as is the range of the Hebrew harp, varied as are its tones, intense as is its action, and spontaneous as is its movement, yet throughout it never teaches, nor suggests, nor implies what is wrong in doctrine or in morals. In the liveliest play of the imagination, in the most soaring flight of dithyrambic fervor, there is a something which keeps the singer from ever transgressing the bounds of reason and truth. Not that the Hebrew poets move in fetters or reel off their strains from a machine. They are the freest of all writers. The whole form and color of their utterances proceed from their personal character and circumstances, and express the direct action of a human soul moved from within and not from without. Yet when subjected to a rigid scrutiny, these lyric outbursts are found to have a correctness and a purity, the like of which has never been seen anywhere else since the world began. The argument is that if this be the fact, then only a supernatural, a divine influence can account for it. And if the songs of sacred Scripture be doctrinally and morally correct, much more must be its prosaic utterances.

# LECTURE II.

## THE DOCTRINE OF GOD IN THE PSALTER.

# LECTURE II.

### THE DOCTRINE OF GOD.

IMPORTANCE OF THIS POINT—THE PSALTER TEACHES THAT GOD IS ONE—DISTINCT FROM THE WORLD—OF INFINITE PERFECTION—HOLY—CONTRAST OF THE GRECIAN HYMNS—OF THE VEDAS—OF THE AVESTAN—NOT A QUESTION OF RACE—CONCLUSION.

THE history of the Christian Church is a history of the development of Christian doctrine. Of development in the natural sense, and not in the non-natural sense in which the word was employed by Dr. Newman in his attempt to justify on this ground all the novelties of modern and mediæval Popery. The whole mind and will of God for human salvation was, as we believe and are sure, recorded in the Scripture, and as such admits of neither diminution nor increase. But the full meaning and explication of particular doctrines was not understood and formulated until, in course of time, reflection, experience, and especially the sharp attacks of errorists, enabled the Church to draw the line accurately between the truth and that which falsely assumed to take its place. Thus was formed what is justly called the historical faith of the Church. Now it is notable that the first article of the common faith which was thus put under fire, and subjected to keen and unsparing criticism, was the doctrine of God. The Ebionite, Gnostic, Manichæan, Arian, Apollinarian, Sabellian, and Tritheistic heresies, all bear witness to the severity of the conflict. Nor is it at all wonderful that strife should begin just here. The object of worship is the first point in all religion. This decides everything else, in the sense that if a man be wrong here, he will be so throughout. If he believe the Deity to be impersonal, or identified with the world, or more than one, or without providence, or limited, or partial, or immoral, all his other beliefs will be modified accordingly. The stream can not rise higher than its fountain, nor can the worshipper be better than the Being whom he worships.

I propose in this lecture to consider what is plainly taught or necessarily implied in the Psalms respecting the being, character, and perfections of God, and then to compare it with the views given in other sacred anthologies, and from the comparison draw such inferences as are fairly deducible.  This course is the more interesting and suggestive, because it does not compare creed with creed, or law with law; does not take up abstract formularies, carefully prepared and guarded, but deals with the actual workings of the religious principle, and shows how men, under the deepest excitements of feeling, conceived and represented Him whom they call God; so that we learn not only what they professed, but what they actually believed, what really entered into and moulded life and character.

(1). The Psalter knows of only one God.  A great variety of names is applied to Him, but it is always one and the same Being that is meant. Some of these names are plural in form, and seem to suggest a plurality of persons in one substance—a suggestion which is further confirmed by the language of the Second Psalm and the One Hundred and Tenth; but however that may be, or whatever explanation of these peculiarities may be adopted, none can question that the unity of the Divine Essence is maintained throughout the entire book.  Mention is indeed made of other gods, but never in the way of recognizing them as having a real existence, but as subsisting only in the vain imaginations of their worshippers. Instead of being considered as actual rivals, they are called false gods, idol gods, no gods. It is true we find no such formal and stately assertions of the divine unity as are given by Moses: "The Lord our God is one Lord" (Deuteronomy vi. 4); or Hezekiah, "Thou art the God, even thou alone, of all the kingdoms of the earth" (2 Kings xix. 15); or Isaiah, "I am the Lord, and there is no God besides me" (xlv. 6); but it is a stronger testimony when we find all the utterances of deep emotion, whether glad or sorrowful, implying, as if unconsciously, or as if it were a matter about which no dispute could exist, that the object of worship is One. No hint is given either of Dualism or Polytheism, although the writers were just as much tempted as any of their neighbors on the East or the West to fall back on these plausible, but superficial, methods of escaping from the difficulties met in understanding the moral government of the world. But while the Hebrew Lyrics maintain thus clearly One God, they also represent Him throughout as—

(2). Distinct from the world. Pantheism is the oldest and at the same time the youngest of religious errors. Its origin is sought among the most ancient traditions of the race, and yet to-day it is professed by not a few, even under the broad blaze of the Christian Revelation. There appears to be something strangely attractive in the conception of one eternal substance of which all that appears from age to age is only a temporary modification. Men do not like either the name or the fact of being atheists, and they take refuge from the disagreeable necessity in a scheme of thought which identifies God and the universe; and yet there is no one but knows that to make everything God, and to say that there is no God, practically amounts to the same thing. All that is useful in Theism is equally done away in both cases. Yet ancient and widespread and enticing as this error is, there is not the least trace of it in the Psalms. They have much to say of God and much to say of His works, but the two are never represented as necessary and constituent parts of one whole. On the contrary, they are sharply distinguished. God, the personal God, is Maker and Ruler, while men and things are the product of His creative hand. "He spake, and it was done; He commanded, and it stood fast" (xxxiii. 9). There are several of what might be called Psalms of Nature, in which there is a detailed description of natural objects; but never is there even a trace of pantheistic thought or expression. Sun and moon, and the stars of light, dragons and all deeps, mountains and all hills, fruitful trees and all cedars, beasts and all cattle, creeping things and flying fowl—in short, the heavens and the earth, and whatever they contain, all, all are creatures of the divine power. "Whatsoever the Lord pleased, that did He in heaven, and in earth, in the seas, and all depths" (cxxxv. 6). The sacred writers are familiar with all the grand or beautiful aspects of the external world which in every age have been the poet's storehouse of images and of sentiment; but we never find anything like the quasi-independence of nature which is disagreeably prominent in modern poets, such as Wordsworth and Bryant. One of the most admired productions of the former is the well-known Tintern Abbey. Who does not remember the fine passage beginning,—

>     For I have learned
> To look on nature, not as in the hour
> Of thoughtless youth; but hearing oftentimes
> The still sad music of humanity,
> Nor harsh, nor grating, though of ample power
> To chasten and subdue.

The poet describes with wonderful strength and beauty the influence of external nature upon the human heart, showing, as does the whole piece, his imaginative force, his spiritual insight, and his power of vivid characterization. "His thoughts are fresh and have the dew on them." Yet at the close he outrages all propriety in saying that he is

> Well pleased to recognize
> In nature, and the language of the sense,
> The anchor of my purest thoughts, the nurse,
> The guide, the guardian of my heart, and soul
> Of all my moral being.

For this is simply to make nature take the place of God to the soul. The poet confounds the soft sensations produced by the beauties of the world of sense, with the moral emotions which the thought of the good God working in them produces. It is every way desirable to "see into the life of things," and to be able to obtain even from the meanest flower that blows "thoughts that do often lie too deep for tears," but it is not at all necessary to call or consider all the emotions awakened by nature, piety. This is a perilous confusion of things that differ. Robertson of Brighton vindicates this passage from the charge of Pantheism by referring to other poems of the author tending in a directly opposite direction, which, of course, are to be taken into account in estimating his position. But in the Psalter there is no need of balancing one portion against another. The Hebrew singers looked upon the earth's fair variety of things with as much kindling imagination and reflective insight as any poet of ancient India or modern England; but never for an instant, or under any circumstances, did they use language which could suggest that they identified the world and its Maker, but just the contrary. For example, in the magnificent storm described in Ps. xxix, which, as Delitzsch says, begins with a *gloria in excelsis*, and ends in a *pax in terris;* every feature—the gathering fury of the elements, the peal of thunder, the flash of the lightning, the crashing cedars, and the quaking mountains—is ascribed directly to the Lord who sits as King forever, and who, controlling the wildest uproar of earth, gives to His people both strength and peace.

The works of the American writer referred to contain an exquisite poem, entitled *Thanatopsis*, written at the age of eighteen, and perhaps unsurpassed by anything produced in the long course of the author's after years. It begins,—

> To Him who in the love of nature holds
> Communion with her visible forms, she speaks
> A various language;

and it proceeds to interpret that language under varying circumstances, especially in reference to the end of life. Yet even the name of God does not once occur. The author was, we know, as he still is, a Christian, yet his verse might have been written by a firm believer in Spinoza or Hegel. I am not finding fault with the poem. Its perfect rhythm, its unity, its sustained thought, its felicities of allusion and expression disarm criticism. And it must be admitted that in other efforts of Mr. Bryant's muse, such as the noble *Forest Hymn*, the theistic recognition is as distinct as any one could desire. But the characteristic of the Psalter is that there are no exceptions to its tone. It holds firmly to the everlasting distinction between the universe and its Creator. All nature is but the expression of God's glory, and it always points to something above and beyond itself. Nor is there a line inconsistent with the lofty utterance at the close of Psalm cii.,—

> Of old hast Thou laid the foundation of the earth,
> And the heavens are the work of Thy hands;
> They shall perish, but Thou remainest,
> Yea, all of them shall wax old as a garment,
> As a vesture shalt Thou change them, and they shall be changed;
> But THOU art the same,
> And Thy years shall have no end.

(3). The God of the Psalter is not only God alone, and distinct from the world, but possessed of infinite attributes. These are sometimes formally stated, at others quietly assumed as the basis of prayer, praise, or devout meditation. We, of course, are familiar with the conception of God as the infinite Spirit in whom all excellence inheres. But the glory of the Psalmists is that, writing when and where they did, they made no mistakes upon the subject. Neither tradition, nor philosophy, nor conceptions borrowed from their neighbors, ever led them to any unworthy representations of the object of worship. Take, for example, the first attribute of Deity which suggests itself to man, that of Power. If God be distinct from the world, then either He made the world, or, what seems to be the natural outcome of the Development Theory when pushed to its legitimate results, the world made God. The Psalmists

have no hesitation here. To them God is
עֶלְיוֹן, the most High, and שַׁדַּי, the Almighty. To
Him none on earth, none in heaven are to be
compared. Strong is His hand, high is His
right hand. The heavens are His, the earth
also is His; as for the world and the fulness
thereof, He has founded them (lxxxix.) He sits
serene upon the flood, yea, He sits as King forever. The power of men, of all creatures, is
necessarily limited. We must use means to accomplish our ends, and patiently contrive expe-
dients to make nature subservient to our purposes. But God wills, and it is done. He ac-
complishes without effort whatever seems good
to Him. As the Thirty-third Psalm says,
"By the word of the Lord were the heavens
made; and all the host of them by the breath
of His mouth." The idea of creation as wrought
either by necessity or by law never seems to
have occurred to the Hebrew singers. All
that is seen is due to One Supreme Personal
Will. "Our God is in the heavens; He hath
done whatsoever He pleased" (cxv. 3).

So also of God's Eternity. There is no attempt at a philosophical explanation of timeless
existence, but a simple distinct assertion that
the Lord is exalted above all the limitations of

time. This indeed is implied in the peculiar, revealed, covenant name, Jehovah—I AM.

The sublime thought of self-existence involves the similar thought of eternity. But the Psalter affirms the truth in direct words:

> Before the mountains were brought forth,
> Or ever Thou gavest birth to the earth and the world,
> Even from everlasting to everlasting Thou art God.
> A thousand years in Thy sight
> Are but as yesterday when it passeth,
> And as a watch in the night.—(xc).

He, therefore, is without beginning of days or end of years. He is, He always has been, He always will be. With Him there is no distinction between the past, the present, and the future. "A thousand years are in Thy sight as yesterday when it is passed." With Him duration is an eternal now. But this thought is uttered not as a mere sentiment, but in living contrast with man's brief, shifting, troubled years, and as an ever-enduring support under the consciousness of human sin and frailty. For which reason the lofty and plaintive Psalm I have quoted is read to-day at a Christian funeral with the same propriety and force as when three thousand years ago men first turned in their sorrow to the Eternal God as a Refuge.

In like manner are we taught respecting God's immensity. He is infinite in relation to space just as He is in relation to time. He is equally present with all His creatures, at all times and in all places. No explanation of the truth is given or attempted, but the fact is set forth with wonderful power and beauty.

> Whither shall I go from Thy Spirit?
> Or whither shall I flee from Thy presence?
> If I ascend into heaven, Thou art there;
> If I make my bed in hell, behold Thou art there.
> If I take the wings of the morning,
> And dwell in the uttermost parts of the sea;
> Even there shall Thy hand lead me,
> And Thy right hand shall hold me.—(cxxxix).

It is true, Calvin says that this passage is wrongly applied to prove the infinite nature of God, for the writer is not concerned with metaphysical conceptions, but with the practical truth, that by no change of place or circumstance can man escape from the eye of God. Undoubtedly the immediate aim is what the great Reformer states, but in reaching this the Psalmist does assert the divine omnipresence, not theoretically, but as an actual fact. And the way in which he does it shows only the more vividly that he does not hold it as a mere abstract dogma, but as a vital truth, powerfully influencing one's heart and life. As God acts everywhere, so is He present everywhere. Spiritual, without form, and therefore invisible, He is present with every blade of grass, every fish of the sea or bird of the air, with every thought of man's heart, with every angel, fallen or elect, with every star in the firmament, with all the works of His hands throughout illimitable space. And as with His presence, so with His knowledge. It is without bounds. Here again we find none of the speculations with which theologians and scholars have wearied themselves in all ages, but simple unambiguous statements, which convey the truth distinctly to the mind of the most unlettered. Indeed, so far from attempting to explain the truth, the writers confess their inability to comprehend it. As we see in the opening of the fine Psalm already quoted.

> O Lord, Thou hast searched me and known me.
> Thou knowest my downsitting and mine uprising ;
> Thou understandest my thought afar off.
> Thou compassest my path and my lying down,
> And art acquainted with all my ways.
> For there is not a word in my tongue,
> But lo, O Lord, Thou knowest it altogether.

Is it any wonder that after this statement of

God's exhaustive knowledge, the Psalmist should add, "Such knowledge is too wonderful for me; it is high, I cannot attain unto it." How can the finite overtake the infinite? Still we can take in and feel the preciousness of the truth that our God is one whose knowledge extends to all the past and all the future, and so can be neither increased nor diminished; to whom the darkness and the light are alike; who knows our thoughts even better than we do ourselves, and who is, therefore, absolutely perfect.

(4). But while the book is thus full and clear upon the natural attributes of the Most High, it is not less, but rather more, distinct and express upon His Moral Perfections. The sum of these is set forth in one word, the frequency and emphasis of which in the Psalms separates them widely from any other so-called Sacred Anthology which the world contains. This is *Holiness*, which is set forth as the peculiar and differentiating characteristic of Jehovah.

> Thou art holy,
> O Thou that inhabitest the praises of Israel.—(xxii. 3).
> Unto Thee will I sing with the harp,
> O Thou Holy One of Israel!—(lxxi. 22).
> Exalt the Lord our God,

And worship at His holy hill,
For He is Holy.—(xcix. 9).
Holy and reverend is His name.—(cxi. 9).

This term denotes entire freedom from moral evil of any and every kind. It is not an excellence in any particular direction, but absolute completeness, and as such it is ascribed to God in the most exclusive terms. Evil can not dwell with Him, the foolish shall not stand in His sight. The utterance of Bildad (Job xxv. 5) on this subject is as true as it is poetical, "Behold even to the moon, and it shineth not; yea, the stars are not pure in His sight." All creatures, even the best, the angels who stand nearest the throne, are mutable in their own nature and limited in their capacities. Holiness in them is but an accident or a quality, but in God it is the very substance of His nature. He is as necessarily holy as He is necessarily God.

This is the fair implication from the language of the sacred poets. And when we look into the peculiar forms in which this essential glory of the divine nature is manifested, the same perfection is to be seen. The Psalmists do not ascribe to God infinite purity in gross, and then take it away in detail. Their teaching is one and the same throughout. Take, *c. g.*, the primary conception which we have of the Supreme Ruler, viz., that He is just. The doctrine is that in all His dealings with His rational creatures He is righteous. His laws are holy and just and good, and these laws are faithfully administered. There is no partiality nor fickleness. God renders to every man according to his works—never condemning the innocent, never clearing the guilty. Now, while it is true that this view must be entertained by any rational theist—for an unjust Supreme God is an unthinkable idea—yet as we all know by observation, if not by experience, there are many things in this world which seem to militate against the equity of the governor of the world. The prosperity of wicked men, and the afflictions of the righteous, apparently, at least, present a constant impeachment of the divine justice. This mournful contrast has always existed as it does now; and it was distinctly recognized by the Psalmists. Nay, they present it not unfrequently with the greatest vividness, and often in the way of earnest complaint. It is the burden of many a prayer, the source of many a painful perplexity. God's providence seems to run counter to His repeated promises, and the pious sufferer is tempted to say, "Verily, in vain have I cleansed my heart, and washed my hands in innocency." But never for one moment is the rectitude of Jehovah questioned. In the darkest hour, when flesh and heart fail, the soul still holds firmly that the Judge of all the earth must do right. Clouds and darkness may be around Him, but righteousness and judgment are the habitation of His throne (xcvii. 2). Nor is the divine righteousness a mere name, but a reality. Jehovah is the God to whom vengeance belongeth. He is angry with the wicked every day. A fire goeth before Him and burneth up His enemies round about (xcvii.) He teareth in pieces, and there is none to deliver (l. 22). No combinations succeed against Him; "He that sitteth in the heavens shall laugh." Nor do any outward professions of rectitude avail; "Unto the wicked He saith, What hast thou to do to declare my statutes, or that thou shouldst take my covenant in thy mouth?" And yet side by side with these assertions of God's strict punitive righteousness are the most ample and express statements of His grace.

> How excellent is Thy loving-kindness, O Lord!—(xxxvi. 7).
> The Lord is good, His mercy is everlasting—(c. 3).

> The Lord is merciful and gracious,
> Slow to anger and plenteous in kindness.
> He will not always chide,
> Neither keep His anger forever.
> For as the heaven is high above the earth,
> So great is His mercy toward them that fear Him.
> —(ciii. 8, 9, 11).

Every reader is familiar with these amiable and winning representations of God. They run through and through the book. And they concur with the sterner utterances before cited to round out one absolutely complete conception—a God, holy yet gracious, just yet merciful. Neither attribute is sacrificed to the other. No one-sidedness is to be seen. In the same collection we have a psalm like the Fiftieth, describing in sublime strains Jehovah's universal judgment, and another, like the One Hundred and Thirty-sixth, where the refrain of every verse is, "His mercy endureth forever." The precise theoretical reconciliation of these perfections could not, of course, be known to the ancient saints as it is to us who live since the Incarnation of the Son of God; but the peculiarity of the case is that, without the flood of light shed by the Gospel, these sacred poets, writing at such different times and places, yet held the balance so even, and set forth an idea of God as men's ruler and judge so well-poised and adequate, that even the New Testament does not alter the lines. The best thoughts of the best Christians toward God are still fully and justly expressed in the words of the old Psalmists—and that not coldly nor dogmatically, but with the energy and fire with which the soul is stirred when it comes to a hand to hand grapple with the great problems of human life and human destiny.

Such, then, is the theology of the Psalter. No mysticism, no vagueness, no confusion, but the clear conception of one infinite and eternal Being; a personal Spirit, who, instead of being of the world or identified with it, is its Maker and Ruler; who has all conceivable perfections; who does according to His own will, at all times and in all places; but who although thus exalted makes Himself known to His creatures, directs their service, accepts their praises, hears their prayers, counts their tears, soothes their sorrows, forgives their sins, quickens their souls, and is their refuge, counsellor, friend and father. And all this, not drawn into a creed, nor arranged in logical formulas, but wrought into the experience and expressed in the words of men under the deepest excitements of feeling.

How came they to give utterance to such a noble and consistent conception of God? Their case stands alone in all the records of ancient times. Other races and nations indeed had their sacred poems, their hymns to the gods, their expression in lyrical form of religious and devotional feeling, but nothing comparable to the strains of David, or Heman, or Asaph. Take the ancient Greeks. We have a small collection of Hymns to the Gods, popularly known as the Minor Homeric Poems, and once supposed to be the work of Homer, but now known to be of a different authorship. The first remark to be made of them is that they are polytheistic. All are addressed to different gods and goddesses, and although they are exquisite productions of the muse, abounding in tenderness, or grace, or humor, and expressed with all the curious felicity of phrase natural to the best poets of Hellas, they have no claim whatever to consideration as utterances of serious devotion. Instead of offering devout worship to one supreme and infinitely exalted, yet gracious Being, they celebrate the power, the wisdom, the adventures, the amours, the pranks of Apollo, or Mercury, or Venus, or Ceres, or Mars, or Bacchus. . The hymn to Aphrodite or

Venus recounts at length her liaison with Anchises, and although an English editor speaks of its instinctive propriety of manner and words, yet I am quite sure it could not be read before any such audience as I now address, much less a promiscuous assembly. So the hymn to Mercury is simply a diverting recital of the exploits of this little born rogue among the dwellers of Olympus—how he stole the oxen of the sun, and what enormous lies he told to Apollo and to Jupiter when charged with his offence. The nearest resemblance to it in modern literature, that I know of, is Moliere's Comedy, entitled *Les Fourberies de Scapin*. And although the hymns to the Delian and the Pythian Apollo do not shock morality so grossly, yet with all their poetic fire and beauty, they display a coarseness of thought and feeling, and an exercise of low earth-born tempers in the immortals, wholly incompatible with the reverence which we instinctively feel to be due to any object of worship. Poetic inspiration is found abundantly in these Homeric hymns, but of any real divine theopneusty there is not a trace. The same thing is true of the Theogony of Hesiod, and the hymns of Callimachus. The whole atmosphere of these poems is as different from that of the Psalter, as jest is from earnest. There is abundance of poetic feeling, of fine imagination, of delicate allusion, and bewitching description, but not a solitary expression of humility, faith, or spiritual aspiration. All is of the earth, earthy.

But let us try the comparison with the productions of the Hindu muse. Within the present century the treasures of the ancient Sanscrit literature have been exhumed from their long grave, and by translation and commentary been made known to English readers. It seems to be satisfactorily made out that a considerable portion of the Rig-Veda — very much the most important and valuable of all the Vedas—must date back to a period between one thousand and fifteen hundred years before Christ, and therefore expresses the earliest thought of the Aryan races upon religious topics. This Veda contains both poetry and prose. The former, the earlier portion, consists of ten books, in which there are more than a thousand separate hymns, all of which are claimed by the Brahmanic authorities to be the result of divine inspiration—the work of the Deity alone, down to the very last line. The whole of these poems has not yet been translated, and perhaps never will be; and much of them, Max Müller says, "Will and must remain to us a dead letter" (*Chips from a German Workshop*, I., 75). "owing to the difficulty of introducing ourselves into the circle of thought and feeling in which these writers so far back, and in such different circumstances habitually moved." Did it not occur to this scholar to ask why we do not have the same difficulty of entering into the Psalmist's circle of thought and feeling? Yet enough has been put into English to enable us justly to estimate the ethical or theological value of the whole. The same writer, a critic neither incompetent nor severe, says, "Large numbers of the Vedic hymns are childish in the extreme; tedious, low, common-place. The gods are constantly invoked to protect their worshippers, to grant them food, large flocks, large families, and a long life; for all which benefits they are to be rewarded by the praises and sacrifices offered day after day, or at certain seasons of the year. But hidden in this rubbish are precious stones," (*Chips*, I., 26). Now it is undeniable that Monotheism is not the doctrine of the Vedas. In numberless cases the hymns are addressed to individual deities, whose names suggest almost irresistibly their

origin from the objects or forces of nature—
*e. g.*, the sun, the earth, the dawn, the storms, the waters, the fire, etc. However beautiful, lofty, or impressive these addresses may at times be, however true it is that the poet, when writing, considered the god he addressed as supreme and absolute, losing all the others from sight; yet the gathering of these different hymns into the same collection produced all the effects of the ordinary polytheism of other lands in degrading the idea of God, and paving the way for the monstrous excesses of idolatry. And if, on some occasions, the Hindu poets rose to the conception of a Supreme mind, transcending all other minds, it was yet identified with nature; so that the whole collection oscillates perpetually between Polytheism and Pantheism. It is true, that sometimes there are ascriptions of praise which remind one of Biblical utterances; as when it is said of Varuna, "Where two persons sit together, he is the third." "The two seas (sky and ocean) are Varuna's loins; he is also contained in this drop of water." "He counts the twinklings of the eyes of men." "As a player throws the dice, he settles all things." "May all thy fatal nooses catch the man who tells the lie, may

they pass by him who tells the truth." (*Chips*, I., 41). There is, too, the recognition of the power and will of the gods to pardon sin : " Varuna is merciful even to him who has committed sin," (p. 40). But for the purpose of comparison, the Veda is to be estimated as a whole. To take selected passages, and from them to infer the character and bearing of the rest, is to fall into the same error as the late Mr. Deutch, who gathered out of the Talmud a number of its most striking things, and left the impression upon his readers, that these fairly represented the immense body of matter contained in a number of folio volumes—the most gigantic accumulation of fable, filth, and trash the world has ever seen.

The same remark is to be made concerning the hymns taken from the Zend-Avesta, the sacred book of a religion justly said to be, of all ethnic faiths, the most admirable for the depth of its philosophy, the spirituality of its views and doctrines, and the purity of its morality. The Zendic Canon is made up of several separate portions differing in age, origin, and character. Hymns of praise are contained in all these, but the most interesting portion is found in the so-called Gathas, five collections of religious lyrics, each collection written in a different metre. The doctrine they hold respecting God is undoubtedly sublime and elevating. There is no worship of nature, no bowing to images, no identification of God with the world; but on the contrary, a distinct recognition of one self-existent and eternal Being who is the Creator of all things. "I invoke," says the Yacma, "Ahura Masda, brilliant, resplendent, greatest and best. All-perfect, all-powerful, all-pure, source of true knowledge, of real happiness; Him who created us, Him who sustains us, wisest of all intelligences." But while this lofty monotheism in form was maintained, while Ahura Masda was held to be the creator and ruler of the universe, and the author of all good; yet, it was also held that there were other sorts of beings who formed a body of malevolent and harmful powers, and from whom came all the wickedness, impurity, and unhappiness in the world. This was the beginning of what afterwards became a fully-developed Dualism, both philosophical and theological. And thus I account for a coldness and vagueness which marks the highest utterances of the Zoroastrian singers. We find bright thoughts, happy sayings, fine descriptions, but nothing like the affectionate, tender, loving confidence which breathes through the Hebrew lyrics. The assurance of the Psalmists that Jehovah was absolutely supreme over all worlds, and that He shared His dominion in no degree, and in no form, with any other beings, was so complete and thorough, that all their reverence and all their hope was toward Him. They, therefore, adopt a tone which, even in the highest flights of imagination, or in the widest reach of poetic license, never loses its sense of complete and all-absorbing devotion to the Being of whom or to whom they sing. While they feared Him as they feared no one else, they loved Him as they loved no one else. It is especially remarkable how they familiarized the thought of God without ever in the least degrading Him in their apprehensions. Some modern Christians, whose sincerity it would be a breach of charity to question, are in the habit of speaking of, and to, their Maker in a tone which is very offensive not merely to a cultivated taste, but to a truly devout soul. It lacks reverence, modesty, delicacy. It forgets the distance between heaven and earth, and treats the Infinite One as if He were a product of clay like themselves. No approach to such an error is found in the Psalter. Its writers bring down the Deity quite within the sphere of human affections, but never impair His majesty. In their most exulting moments they are always reverent, and the object of their hope, and trust, and joy, however tenderly and affectionately addressed, is still to them God—the God whose greatness is unsearchable, and whose understanding is infinite.

The question, then, arises, How came these Hebrews to get and retain the conception of one supreme, personal God, infinitely great, yet infinitely condescending? The answer given by Mons. Renan, who, however we may repudiate his philosophy, is anything but contemptible as a scholar, is that the whole question is one of race. The Semitic family, he says, had the monotheistic instinct, and this accounts for their constant faith in one God alone. But such a theory is every way untenable. For, in the first place, as a matter of fact polytheism is found among the majority of the Semitic races. It prevailed in the Arabian tribes, in Philistia and Phœnicia, and in Syria and Mesopotamia. Among these, the sun, the moon, the planets, and all the host of heaven, as well as other forces of nature, were deified and worshipped. It is only in one branch of the race that we find

Monotheism maintained. Besides, the answer itself needs explanation. The instinct of the irrational animals we understand as the working of the nature given to them, but how can men have an instinct unless implanted by their Creator? Moreover, an instinct is invariable. How came this instinct, if such it were, to be so often utterly denied and extirpated, and that, not for a short period, but for generations and ages? But the whole theory is baseless. Its consideration only brings out more broadly the point aimed at in this lecture. All over the ancient world was Polytheism or Dualism. The Aryan races and the Semitic races alike fell into the monstrous error. It pervades all their literature, whether in hieroglyph, or cuneiform, or ordinary script, and was set forth in pictures and images. But there is one exception, only one, *i. e.*, the Hebrews. And here it is found only in their literature. As for the people themselves, they displayed a constant tendency to go after other gods—not for the most part exchanging Jehovah for a heathen deity, which they did only in the days of Ahab and Jezebel, but taking this deity into partnership with Jehovah. This disposition runs through all their history from the days of Jacob down to the Captivity in

Babylon. That history has justly been said "to be made up of an almost uninterrupted series of relapses into polytheism." And yet this fact left no stamp upon their poetry. The sacred singers never for an instant give way to the error, or even assert the truth in a wavering or uncertain manner. In the height of joy, one God is praised; in the depth of gloom, one God is supplicated. Other gods are mentioned only to be disparaged or denied. Nature is frequently and grandly described, but always as the creature of God. The events of the past are often recounted, but never as results of destiny or caprices of fortune, but as the manifested will of One whose throne is in the heavens, and whose kingdom ruleth over all. Whence came this remarkable peculiarity subsisting through a thousand years? Surely not from the efforts of the Jews themselves, their grasp of intellect or stretch of speculation. Of all the ancient nations they were the least endowed with the philosophic spirit. Neither their language nor their character fitted them for the minute inquiries and subtle distinctions which abounded among the flower of the Aryan races. And yet they held fast with an unyielding grasp a truth which eluded the laborious culture of Athens and

Alexandria. But in fact they never pretended that their idea of the one supreme God was a discovery of their own. "He made known His ways unto Moses, His acts unto the children of Israel." The historical Psalms go back to Abraham (cv. 6) as the head of the race, and refer all the distinctions of the people to the revelation made to him and his successors. This, I say, is their account of the origin of their knowledge of God, and it is the only account which fully meets the requirements of the case. God Himself segregated this race from the children of men, and made them the depositories of His truth, confirming and upholding the original disclosure by continual subsequent communications, from time to time, and thus guarding against the corruptions to which all human institutions are liable. Only in this way can we explain the marvellous purity, and beauty, and consistency of the doctrine of God set forth in the old Hebrew Psalms. Beyond all question these Psalms are human, but equally beyond question are they Divine. The brightest gem in the whole range of addresses to the Gods, found in Greek literature, is the Hymn of the Stoic Cleanthes, addressed to Jupiter, which does really contain some fine thoughts and sounding phrases. But the entire hymn is a splendid illusion. "Stoic dogma empties Stoic hymnology of half its sublimity and more than half its devoutness." The Father in heaven whom Cleanthes praises, and to whom he prays, is not a personal Being, all-righteous and all-holy, whose loving care may be aptly symbolized by the tenderness of an earthly parent, but is only another name for nature, for necessity, for fate, for the universe. The stately words which the writer uses are employed only in a forced and unnatural sense. But the Psalmists always mean just what they say, or if there is any difference, it is because words can not express the fulness and vigor of their thought. In no case do they use language transcending their own feelings and conceptions. And there are scores of these sacred songs as much superior to Cleanthes' Hymn as this is to the Minor Homeric Poems. How is it that the singers of an obscure and despised nation, whom the classic races stigmatized as barbarous, and who, in the arts of life, in all the mental and social habits which lead to depth and breadth of thought, or to the sense and creation of beauty, *were* barbarous in the comparison, yet produced the only conception of God which, by the general consent of the wise and good, is pronounced to be just, and true, and satisfying? The people were merciless and bloody; they were constantly prone to the coarsest irreligion and profligacy, yet their sacred singers express thoughts about God which have been welcomed and adopted by the gentlest, the most refined, and the most saintly spirits whom the world has ever seen. How is this to be accounted for? No answer can be given which does not affirm a divine guidance which controlled thought, and tongue, and pen.

# LECTURE III.

THE DOCTRINE OF MAN IN THE PSALTER.

# LECTURE III.

## THE DOCTRINE OF MAN.

MAN'S ORIGIN AND PLACE IN NATURE—EIGHTH PSALM—HIS MORAL CORRUPTION—THIS UNKNOWN TO OTHER SINGERS—THE REASON OF THE FACT—THE PSALTER PRAISES GOD AND NOT MAN—NO MYTHICAL IDEALS OF HUMANITY—NO PESSIMISM—LOFTY FAITH IN GOD AND ATTACHMENT TO HIM—NO CLANNISHNESS—HOPE FOR THE WORLD—THIS NOW A COMMON PLACE, NOT SO THEN—CONCLUSION.

IN the last lecture the subject was the teaching of the Psalter respecting God, His nature and attributes, and His relations to men. This point naturally came first, because it is first—being the pivot upon which all other truths turn. But next to the question of God, comes that of man. How is he regarded as to his position in the world—his origin, his character, his duty, and his destiny. This constitutes the other factor in any scheme of religious thought, and is worthy of the most attentive consideration. What, then, is the doctrine of the Psalms on this point? Is it like that of other religious systems? Does it start on the same plane and arrive at the same end? or does it differ widely, and if so, how shall we account for the difference?

The first inquiry respects man's origin and his place in creation. The general doctrine of antiquity on this subject was that man is a spontaneous production of the earth, since almost all philosophers held that matter was eternal, on the ground *ex nihilo nihil fit*—the idea of creation seeming to them unphilosophical and incredible. The earth was assumed to be pregnant with the germs of all living organisms, which were quickened into life under favorable circumstances. Hence the great boast of the Athenians was that they were not derived from any other existing race, but αυτοκθονες, sprung from the soil. It is true, we have what seems a contrary doctrine in the statement quoted by Paul in his address on Mars' Hill at Athens, Τοῦ γὰρ καὶ γένος ἐσμέν, whether we suppose this fine utterance taken from Aratus of Cilicia, (270 B.C.) or from the famous hymn of Cleanthes, the Stoic. But these were mere sporadic utterances, and besides were rather used to show that God was like to man than that man was like to God. The former view being the prolific parent of idolatry in its grossest forms, while the latter, as handled by the great Apostle, furnishes the most emphatic protest against such a degrading habit.

In the Psalms, on the contrary, the position long before taken in Genesis—that man was made, and that he was made in the image of God—is everywhere assumed, and sometimes explicitly formulated and poetically developed. As in the 100th Psalm, "Know ye that the LORD He is God: it is He that hath made us and not we ourselves: we are His people and the sheep of His pasture." Still more vividly is this set forth in the 8th Psalm, where David gives feeling expression to the insignificance of man in the presence of the vastness, the splendor, the mysterious depth and the boundless glory of the heavens, as seen at night.—

> When I see Thy heavens, the work of Thy fingers,
> The moon and the stars which Thou hast ordained;
> What is man, that Thou art mindful of him,
> And the son of man, that Thou visitest him?

As Dr. Whewell says, "The vault of the sky arched at a vast and unknown distance over our heads; the stars apparently infinite in number, each keeping its appointed course and place, and seeming to belong to a wide system which has no relation to the earth; while man is but one among many millions of the earth's inhabitants, all this makes the contemplative spectator feel how exceeding small a portion of the universe he is; how little he must be in the eyes of an Intelligence which can embrace the whole." And it may well be doubted whether the brilliant discoveries of modern astronomy cause the view of the nightly heavens to make any deeper impression upon a modern spectator than it did upon the sweet singer of Israel ages ago. Even we can hardly say with more emotion than David, What is man in the sight of Him who made those heavens, and in them planted those glittering orbs? But no sooner does the poet give utterance to the thought of man's insignificance on this side of the subject, than he turns to set forth on the other, his wondrous greatness — in nature almost divine, crowned and sceptered as a king, wielding a dominion over air and earth, and seas — all things put under his feet. The first theme of the lyric is the manifested excellence of the Creator, so conspicuously displayed in all the earth, and in the heavens above the earth, as to attract the admiration of children, and even sucklings. But the second is the dignity of man, made by the favor of God to be the head of creation, animate and inanimate. Little as he is in one sense, in another he is inexpressibly great—nothing less than a sovereign ruler like his Maker and Lord. Thus was anticipated in the old Hebrew song, the fine thought of Pascal—" Man is but a reed, the weakest in nature, but he is a thinking reed. It is not necessary that the entire universe arm itself to crush him. A breath of air, a drop of water, suffices to kill him. But were the universe to crush him, man would be still more noble than that which kills him, because he knows that he dies; and the universe knows nothing of the advantage it has over him."

But while the Psalms wholly ignore all theories of man as an emanation or a development, and set him on the pinnacle of the earth as a creature bearing the lineament of the divine handiwork; yet on the other hand they are far from affirming that his moral character is in accordance with his origin and his place in nature. Nay, they declare just the reverse. In the Epistle to the Romans, the Apostle sets forth his grand indictment against the race— that Jews and Gentiles are all alike under sin —and then rivets his conclusion by citations from Scripture—"it is written," giving a cento of six different passages. Four of these are from the Psalter. It will suffice to quote the most striking of them—the opening of the 14th Psalm, which is also the same as that of the 53d—a case of repetition or *retractatio*, which is well justified by the importance of the theme, and the indisposition of men to receive it.

The fool hath said in his heart, There is no God.
They are corrupt, they have done abominable works.
There is none that doeth good.
The LORD looked down from heaven upon the children of men,
To see if there be any that understand,
That seek after God.
They are all gone aside, they are together become filthy,
There is none that doeth good, no, not one.

The Psalmist, doubtless, had an historical occasion for this utterance, although we can not determine what it was. But rising above any particular circumstances, he surveys the whole race and brands it with a fatal apostasy. Even the eye of the Omniscient, looking down from the height of heaven, fails to discern a single sinless person. Well says Ewald, "It would scarcely be possible for a great truth to be sketched in fewer or more striking outlines." Yet the subject is not always treated in this objective way. Generally, it comes out, as we should expect in lyrics, as a matter of experience. There is no reference in all the Psalter to the origin of evil, or to our connection with the head of the race. But the deep doctrine of depravity, as hereditary, inborn, and all-pervading, is distinctly set forth. In Psalm lviii. 3, David traces the corruption of his times back to original sin, to an evil germ infecting the nature even from birth. "The wicked are estranged from the womb: they go astray as soon as they be born, speaking lies." Still more affectingly is the same assertion made by him in regard to himself in Psalm li. 5, when bewailing the great transgression of his life. Not content with acknowledging his actual misdeeds, he goes back to the fountain from which they sprang—a corrupt nature. "Behold, I was shapen in iniquity, and in sin did my mother conceive me." This is not said in extenuation of his conduct, but in aggravation of it—not as casting blame upon his mother—the shocking hypothesis which some writers have allowed themselves to frame—but as affirming that the poison of sin, instead of being restricted to particular wrong acts, however many or gross, went down to the roots of his being, and affected the whole life and character. Not that this took away guilt as if sin were an involuntary thing, for man's responsibility is constantly assumed—being given in this very Psalm as clearly as it is in every human consciousness. Need I recite other touching utterances,—

> If thou, Lord, shouldst mark iniquities,
> O Lord, who should stand?—(cxxx.)

Or again,—

> Enter not into judgment with thy servant,
> For in thy sight shall no man living be justified.—(cxliii.)

All, all need His pardoning mercy, and this not only for known, but unknown sins. "Who can discern His errors? Cleanse Thou me from secret faults." These sayings are not due to poetic license or rhetorical exaggeration, but are the true utterances of a deep and real feeling. And as such they stand alone in literature. Nowhere in the sacred anthology of Rome, Greece, Assyria, Persia, Hindustan, or China, do we find any equivalent to it. Not that these peoples were ignorant of the fact of human depravity and of its extent. How could they be? What they saw within and around them, and all the records of the past, compelled them to feel and acknowledge that human nature was in a sad, disjointed condition. Philosophers could find no explanation of the universal fact save in the idea of a general rooted depravity of the race. And many a poet has, like Ovid, deplored the inward conflict between inclination and conscience—the clear perception of what is right, and yet the determined following of what is wrong. But all these utterances were more matters of speculation than of emotion. They were not so held by men as to shape their religious convictions, or to govern their worship or their lives. The nearest approach I have seen to the Scripture utterance is in some of the Hindu hymns, of which the following is a specimen:

"I am sin, I commit sin, my nature is sinful, and I am conceived in sin.
Save me, O thou lotus-eyed, O Hari, who removest all sin."

These words have a very orthodox sound, and, being the daily prayer of the Brahmans, while performing their religious ablutions, have often been quoted to them by Christian missionaries as asserting the great truth which renders the sacrifice of the Cross so needful and so precious. But neither did the ancient authors of this prayer, nor do those who incessantly repeat it now, mean by its words what it seems to us to say. Their philosophy attributes all the pain, the unsatisfied desire, the gloom and misery of human life, to the connection of soul with nature. The spirit is in bondage to matter, and the only prospect of emancipation lies in an enormous series of successive transmigrations until at last it passes into the Supreme source—that is, God. It is easy to see that in this view the most complete and exhaustive confessions of sinfulness have a very different meaning from that which the same words express when used by believers in the Bible. The moral corruption which the Hindu bewails is not the consequence of his own act, or that of his legal representative, but of dispositions originating in the first construction of the body from the subtle elements of nature. It is, of course, impossible that the sense of responsibility should be keen, or the reproaches of conscience severe. Nor is it surprising that men should come to believe that the sin which owes its being to the body is removed by mere bodily or external observances. A chief feature of the every-day worship of all Brahmans is to bathe in one of the sacred rivers, and while in the act, to repeat the prayer above cited. Their worship and their lives show that they have no proper conception of inbred corruption as this is felt by Christians. Their confessions, so mortifying in terms, are made without either shame or sorrow—indeed for the most part repeated merely as a matter of form. As Dean Church remarks, (*Early Sacred Poetry*, p. 30), "Though in these ancient hymns sin is confessed and its consequences deprecated, though they praise the righteous and denounce the deceitful and the wicked, there is but little to show what was the sin, and what constituted the righteousness. Of that moral conviction, that moral enthusiasm for goodness and justice, that moral hatred of wrong and evil, that zeal for righteousness, that anguish of penitence which has elsewhere marked religious poetry, there is singularly little trace."

It may, then, be fairly affirmed that the ethnic faiths scarcely understood the strict idea of sin as an offence against God. They had no inkling of that view of the Divine Holiness which pervades the Scriptures, and which was continually and strongly represented in a tangible shape to Israel, alike by the minute and painful symbolism of the ceremonial institute; by the stern and unbending enactments of the moral law; and by the actual and repeated judgments God sent both upon them and upon their heathen neighbors in upholding the Law. Even in the master-pieces of Greek Tragedy, the Nemesis is not so much the result of the deliberate purpose of a supreme divine person as the acting of a blind unconscious Fate to which gods and men are alike subject. There is a plenty of pathos, of terror, of wrong-doing, and of ultimate suffering, but never once the spiritual conception of sin as a disease of the moral nature needing both pardon and renovation in order to free the conscience from its load. And why? How comes it that the varied and cultivated races with an ancestral faith, with an elaborate cultus, and with a very striking mental development, never, save in very rare instances, looked deep enough into their own hearts to see what was there, while these Hebrew singers had such a vivid conception of the truth, and expressed it with such feeling and power, and never set forth any statements of an opposite kind? It is no answer to ascribe this effect to the moral earnestness of the Hebrew race. For first, the other races had as much earnestness, only they showed it in a different way. When did any people fall into such a paroxysm of dismay, terror, and wrath, as the Athenians at the mutilation of the Hermæ; or as the Egyptians, when Cambyses mocked at their sacred customs? What people could be more earnest in their religion than those Syrian tribes who made their children pass through the fire to Moloch? But, secondly, if they did not have it, it remains to be explained how the Hebrews alone came to be in possession of it. The only possible solution is, I submit, to be found in the direct and specific divine revelation which they enjoyed, and which, by furnishing the pure and lofty standard of duty, enabled men to ascertain exactly their deviations from it.

This view of human nature gave rise to another peculiarity by which the Hebrew Lyrics are distinguished, viz.: that their praise is always of God or of God's works, and never of man. The earlier history of the race abounds with men of remarkable character: the innocent Abel; the unworldly Enoch; the faithful Noah; the mysterious Melchizedek; Abraham, the friend of God; the contemplative Isaac; Jacob, the wrestler and prince; Joseph with his diversified and romantic history; Moses, the law-giver, with his wondrous career from the bulrushes of the Nile to the lonely summits of Nebo; Aaron, the head of the oldest priesthood in the world;

Joshua, the great captain; Jephthah and Gideon, the mighty men of valor; and Samuel, last of the judges and first of the prophets. These names were rooted in the hearts and the memories of their countrymen, and all regarded them with a glow of national pride.

Why do not these appear in the song-book of the nation? Why do we not find some encomiastic, or triumphal, or elegiac odes in honor of these distinguished men? Why in all the Psalter is there nothing in this respect even approaching the sublime odes in which Pindar immortalized the victors at the great games of Greece? That the fact is as I have stated, is indisputable. There is not a psalm of praise in the entire collection which has for its chief, or even its subordinate, subject, the exploits of any man or set of men. The spirit of the whole is faithfully expressed by the opening words of the 115th Psalm, "Not unto us, O Lord, not unto us, but unto Thy name give glory, for Thy mercy, for Thy truth." It may, perhaps, be said that all poems of this kind were recorded in the book of Jasher, or of the Upright, which is mentioned in Joshua x. 13, and 2 Samuel i. 18, and of which nothing is certainly known, although for ages its precise nature has been a theme of laborious disputation. To me the opinion of Lowth appears most probable—that it was a collection of national songs, celebrating either the civil or the military exploits of the great men of the past. But admitting this to be the fact in the case, the question at issue is pushed only a step farther back. For supposing these two collections to be growing up side by side, how came it to pass that the secular never even by chance invaded the sacred, but the line of demarkation was kept distinct from beginning to end? And why was it that the one perished so entirely that we know not of its existence at all, except by two slight references in the canonical Scriptures, while the other was at once taken into the canon, and has so remained for ages an integral part of the Hebrew Scriptures? Certainly this is not the ordinary course of events. Pride of ancestry and pride of race are universal features of human nature. We find them in all modern, in all ancient literatures—in the lyrics of Greece and Rome, in the hymns of the Veda, in the Gâthâs of the Avestan, in the cuneiform inscriptions of Chaldea and Assyria. If, then, the book of Jasher was what it is commonly supposed to be, it only makes the case stronger. The Hebrews did not omit to preserve songs in praise of illustrious men, because they had none of that class; but on the contrary, having them and enough of them to make a "book," they yet refused to mingle them with the songs of Zion, and kept their sacred anthology pure from even the least taint of hero worship, or saint worship. This is clearly established by one signal case. On the death of Saul and Jonathan, David composed one of the most exquisite elegies of any age or land. It is recorded in the second book of Samuel (i. 17-27) as part of the annals of the time, and as useful in many directions. But it was not put into the Psalter, it was not inscribed "To the chief musician." Neither its author, nor its subject, nor its occasion, nor its inherent beauties of thought and expression, could gain for it admission into that collection whose title is *Thehillim*—Praises, the Praises of God. Nor may it be said that there were not in Jewish history events or scenes sufficiently striking to be embalmed in poetic numbers. The record proves the contrary abundantly. The material existed, but some unseen force hindered the singers from using it in any such way as would turn men's thoughts from their Maker's honor to the glorification of mere men, as may be seen by comparing the treatment of a celebrated modern feat of arms with that of a similar one of old. The brilliant exploit of the British cavalry at Balaklava has been worthily perpetuated in Tennyson's Charge of the Light Brigade, and multitudes who otherwise might never have heard of the brave deed, will know it well from the poet's striking lyric. But the three captains who broke through the garrison at the well of Bethlehem did quite as glorious an enterprise in snatching at the risk of life a cup of water for David, and their self-sacrifice was even surpassed by the generous devotion of their leader, but not the remotest allusion to it occurs in the Psalter.

Still further, not only is there no attempt at the glorification of real personages in the national history, but no appearance of an effort after an ideal of humanity, a mystic conception of what is greatest and best according to earthly standards. Among every cultivated people it has been a favorite object of men of genius to give expression to some faultless model of the race, to paint a perfect picture of godlike virtue, wisdom, courage, self-control, and endurance, and to hold this up for imitation and admiration. In all such poems it is required that they be true to human nature generically, but not in detail. They borrow indeed from actual history, but they add and omit, and expand and diversify, until they have finally created their ideal character. But however skilfully drawn, whatever excellence the work has in tone, style, and structure, it is only a romance. It may have the highest possible verisimilitude, but still no objective truth. "No such embodiment of the Ideal has ever broken in upon the vulgar realities of human existence. There have been good men, and brave men, and wise men, often; but there have been no living sculptures after the fashion of Phidias, no heroes after the manner of Homer and Virgil." Nothing of this kind appears in the Psalter. It is as free from any imaginary or mythical heroes as from any that are historical. Its whole atmosphere is that of literal truth—reciting of men, even the best of men, their shame as well as their glory, their sins, and falls, and infirmities as well as their faith, and heroism, and devotion. The only apparent exception to this uniformity is the reference to one described sometimes as a king, at others as a prophet, who is indeed set forth as invested with every possible excellence. But this is not a real exception. For although a certain school of Rationalists have endeavored to account for these passages, and others in the rest of the Old Testament, as representing an ideal Christ, an earth-born conception of men dissatisfied with what they saw around them, and therefore striving to give a concrete picture of what they hoped would be developed in the progress of society, the attempt has signally failed. The theory is totally inadequate to answer its purpose, as might be easily shown were there time. And the old view remains impregnably established—that this lyric hero, so far from being of human invention, is of divine suggestion. He is the great hope of Israel, a real personage who in the fulness of time should appear to bridge the chasm between heaven and earth by a wondrous Incarnation. Upon the glories of this Being the sacred singers exhaust all their stores. But the bright portraiture they give of Him only displays the more clearly their absolute restraint from any degree or form of panegyric upon a mere man.

But while the Psalms are free from all secular, eulogistic songs in praise of individuals, and while they freely speak of the whole race as in a lost and sinful condition, they are far from any pessimistic extravagance. There is none of the hopelessness of heathenism or mere nature. Men have gone astray, but they may be recovered. They are burdened with guilt, but that burden may be shifted. They are banished from God, yet they may be brought back to His fellowship. For along with the clearest statements of human sin, we have similar statements of the divine mercy. "The Lord is merciful and gracious, slow to anger and plenteous in kindness. He will not always chide, neither keep His anger forever." In consequence of this, penitents have hope. And it is these repeated, express, and emphatic affirmations of the divine compassion which distinguish the Psalms from the Vedas and the Avestan. What in the latter is set forth vaguely, rarely, and hesitatingly, in the former is triumphantly assumed and made the basis of prayer and assurance. A conspicuous instance is seen in the 103d Psalm:

> He hath not dealt with us after our sins,
> Nor rewarded us according to our iniquities.
> For as the heaven is high above the earth,
> So great is His mercy toward them that fear Him.
> As far as the east is from the west,
> So far hath He removed our transgressions from us.
> Like as a father pitieth his children,
> So the Lord pitieth them that fear Him.
> For He knoweth our frame;

> He remembereth that we are dust.
> For the wind passeth over it, and it is gone,
> And the place thereof shall know it no more;
> But the mercy of the Lord is from everlasting to everlasting upon them that fear Him,
> And His righteousness unto children's children.

In consequence of such utterances as these, the singers of old, without having the full-orbed doctrine of atonement as it lies in the New Testament, were able to apprehend God as gracious and forgiving, and yet to feel His grace, not as a license to sin, but as a fresh bond to duty. As one of them said, "There is forgiveness with Thee that Thou mayest be feared." The forgiveness takes away the estrangement wrought by sin, and the soul comes back to its old place as a child of God and a sharer in His image. It loves Him, it serves Him, it enjoys Him. His statutes are more precious than gold, sweeter than the honey-comb. It meditates therein by day and by night. Its cry is, "Because thou hast been my help, therefore in the shadow of Thy wings will I rejoice." "How precious also are Thy thoughts unto me, O God? How great is the sum of them! If I should count them, they are more in number than the sand; when I awake, I am still with Thee."

Now, this is a phase of experience to which all ancient literature has nothing that even approaches an analogy. It may be said of some of the hymns of the Veda that their writers were seekers after God, but they were not finders. The highest idea they formed of what God could bestow was earthly, temporal blessings—life, health, riches, success. Whereas, in the Psalms we have a conception of the true blessedness of the human soul, not surpassed even in the New Testament. They seem to have anticipated the fine saying of Augustine—"Thou hast made us for Thyself, and our heart hath no rest until it rest in Thee." See in the 16th Psalm—"The Lord is the portion of my inheritance and my cup." Not what He gives or promises, but Himself. He is more and better than all His gifts. Just as the eye was formed for light, and the ear for sound, and the intellect for truth—and these organs can find pleasure only in their respective objects—so the soul was formed by God for Himself, and can never know real and abiding enjoyment except in Him. This undertone runs all through the Psalter, but sometimes comes to the surface in a very striking way. "There be many that say, who will shew us any good?" (iv. 6).

Yes, for centuries after David, this was the burden of every philosophical inquiry, and many, many have been the answers; yet, none has superseded His own simple and all-sufficient utterance—" Lord, lift Thou up the light of Thy countenance upon us."

So, again, in the very remarkable Psalm of Asaph, in which the saint finds his faith staggered at seeing the prosperity of the wicked. Their eyes stand out with fatness, and they have more than heart could wish. It seems, therefore, as if all the pains of God's people have been thrown away. In vain have they washed their hands in innocency. But going into the Sanctuary, he sees their latter end, how they are brought to desolation as in a moment, and all their prosperity vanishes like a dream. And thus the apparent mystery of Providence is explained. But there is more than this. The holy singer reaches a far higher point. Even supposing that there were no such deadly retribution as he has been informed of, there is no need for him to envy the felicities of the wicked. The objects which they seek, and prize, and enjoy, are not what the believer needs. He has far more and better.

> Whom have I in heaven but Thee?
> And upon earth I desire none besides Thee.
> My flesh and my heart faileth;
> But God is the strength of my heart and my portion forever.

As Ewald says—"Though all else in heaven and earth should fail, the one true everlasting Friend abides." Has devout thought in any age ever soared to a loftier eminence? Asaph does not fall into the Pantheistic abyss of the east, nor into the mystical absorption of the west; but maintaining distinctly the Divine Personality and his own, yet finds in the friendly union of the two, the reliance of a finite soul upon an infinite God—all that his heart can wish or his mind conceive. The book which contains that thought came from God.

But was this high privilege confined only to the race to which belonged the men who set it forth? Such a question has often been answered in the affirmative. There are many who speak disparagingly of the Old Testament, on the ground of its restricted views and morose spirit, charging it with what they call a "narrow particularism," meaning by that a scornful antipathy toward the rest of mankind. Now, it is certainly true that the Psalms recognize and celebrate with grateful praise the preeminence which God gave to Israel over other nations. How could they omit to confess what they owed to Him who had chosen them to be His covenant people, who had given them the revelation of His will, and manifested His gracious presence in the Sanctuary? Hence, we read often such utterances as,—

> In Judah is God known,
> His name is great in Israel.—(lxxvi. 2).

> He made known His ways to Moses,
> His acts unto the children of Israel.—(ciii. 7).

> He declared to Jacob His word.
> His statutes and judgments to Israel.
> He hath not dealt so with any nation ;
> And His judgments, they know them not.—(cxlvii. 19, 20).

Yet, it is observable that these statements are never made with any appearance of self-complacency, as if God's favors to them were bestowed as the reward of their own merit, but rather as incitements to thankfulness and praise and holy living. And so far from cherishing a narrow, clannish spirit, they are constantly on the outlook for the time when the blessings they enjoy shall become the common possession of the race. Indeed, the spirit of the Psalms is but an expansion of what is given in the call of Abraham. He was segregated from his kindred, and made the recipient of a special revelation. But why? The very words of the promise indicate the world-wide scope of the arrangement—"In thy seed shall all the families of the earth be blessed." So the sacred singers believed, and so they sang. The contrast between them, and all other singers on this point, has often been remarked. In every literature we find the tradition of a golden age. Men see so much of confusion and darkness in the moral order of the world in their own day, that the heart turns longingly to the conception of a nobler and better state of things in which truth and right shall prevail, and justice accomplish its perfect work. But invariably the ethnic religions placed the blessed period of rest and peace in the past, when the human race was young. Here only did they find any basis for their visions, for when they undertook to forecast the future, it always seemed as if the world were waxing worse and worse. Not only so. They had no idea of the solidarity of the race. That is a conception due only to the Scriptures. The first approach to it was made in the time of Alexander the Great, who, by his vast conquests in Asia, and his endeavors to unify his empire by assimilating Europeans and Asiatics, gave to thoughtful men the notion of a universal history. It is no wonder, therefore, that the heathen contemporaries of our Psalmists never looked forward to a universal reign of righteousness — never solaced the troubles of the present by glancing into the future. The whole conception lay outside of their sphere of thought. So much the more wonderful is it that the singers of a small secluded people, shut off from all others by the great sea on one hand, and the trackless desert on the other, and still more separated by an elaborate ritual which penetrated all points of character and usage, should yet lift themselves bodily out of these restrictions and widen their sympathies to take in all the children of men everywhere. That they did so, is beyond question. The connections in which they gave utterance to this expectation of the universal prevalence of truth and righteousness are manifold and various. Sometimes it is in the flush of some great victory, the experience of which suggests the thought of a far more glorious manifestation of Jehovah's victorious energy. For example, in Psalm xlvii., usually thought to have originated in Jehoshaphat's triumph over Ammon and Edom, the poet begins,—

> O clap your hands, all ye peoples ;
> Shout unto God with the voice of triumph,

thus summoning the whole gentile world to join in the praise. Then, after reciting God's doings, he concludes with predicting an assembly of the nations to do homage as vassals of their one Liege-lord and King :

> The princes of the peoples are gathered together,
> A people of the God of Abraham,
> For unto God belong the shields of the earth.

So again in the remarkable 68th Psalm, after recounting God's blessings in the wilderness, under the judges, and at the foundation of the monarchy, David sees in these only the foreshadowings of a mightier and far more extensive conquest :

> Because of thy temple at Jerusalem
> Kings shall bring presents unto thee.
>
> Princes shall come out of Egypt,
> Ethiopia shall eagerly stretch out her hands unto God :
> Kingdoms of the earth, sing unto God :
> Sing praises unto the Lord.
>
> Ascribe ye strength unto God,
> Over Israel is His majesty,
> And His strength in the clouds.

This does not mean simply a subjugation of the heathen world for Israel's glory, but a subjection which should justly excite the joyful praises of all thus brought into the fellowship of truth. The same prospect is still more distinctly set forth in the 87th Psalm, occasioned by Hezekiah's victory over Sennacherib. After an outburst celebrating the glory of Zion as the city of God, the poet proceeds to describe her brilliant prospects, introducing God as enumerating among His willing people those who had always been fierce enemies of His cause.

> I will mention Rahab and Babylon as them that know me.
> Lo, Philistia and Tyre with Ethiopia.
> (Of each of these it shall be said),
> This one was born there (*i. e.*, in Zion).

Not individuals merely, but whole peoples are to be subjects of regenerating grace. And when Jehovah makes out the muster-roll of His nations, each of these shall find a place in the registry. Well may such an issue be commemorated by a triumphal procession, headed by the singers and the players, saying, "All my springs are in thee."

Another class of Psalms looking to the universal diffusion of the truth, is found in the little fasciculus, comprising xciii.–c., which seem intended in times of darkness and doubt to raise the thoughts of the people up to the Lord as King, who will one day come forth to show His boundless power and authority. The floods lift up their voice, but far above the crash of their foaming billows is the Lord on high (xciii.)

> He is a great God and a great King above all Gods.—(xcv.)
> Give unto the Lord, ye families of nations,
> Give unto the Lord glory and strength.
> Let the sea roar and the fulness thereof;
> The world and they that dwell therein.
> Let the floods clap their hands,
> Let the hills be joyful together
> Before the Lord: for He cometh to judge the earth:
> With righteousness shall He judge the world
> And the peoples with equity.

Sea and land, rivers and mountains, are all summoned to praise in concert God's assumption of His universal sovereignty. Then the series concludes in Psalm 100, with an invitation to the entire race to draw near,—

> Shout unto the Lord, all the earth.
> Serve the Lord with gladness,
> Come before Him with singing.
> Know that the Lord He is God,
> It is He that made us,
> And not we ourselves.

Here are no local restrictions, no national exclusiveness, but a summons to every kindred and tribe, on the ground that Jehovah is the one common Creator and Father of all.

The same largeness of view is found in two other Psalms, very different in their origin and tone, the 102d and 67th. The former, justly entitled a prayer of the afflicted, begins with the description of a sad and bitter lot, but suddenly the writer rises above his sorrows with the thought that God sits as King forever. This divine majesty will one day be manifested on Zion's behalf, and that so signally that nations shall fear the name of Jehovah, and all kings of the earth His glory. Not only that, but peoples and kingdoms shall be gathered together to unite with Israel in recounting Jehovah's praise, and doing His will. In the latter Psalm all this comes out so strikingly, that it has been called the Mission Hymn of the Hebrew Church. It is apparently a harvest song in which the devout singer takes occasion, from the recent experiences of God's goodness in sending a fruitful season, to entreat and to anticipate the extension of the divine bounties to all the nations of the earth.

> God be merciful to us and bless us,
> And make His face to shine upon us.

Why? Mark the large and generous words which immediately follow:

> That Thy way may be known upon the earth,
> Thy saving health among all nations.
> Let the peoples praise Thee, O God,
> Let all the peoples praise Thee.
>
> God even our own God, shall bless us.
> God shall bless us,
> And all the ends of the earth shall fear Him.

Visions like these of universal peace and joy have now become the common property of man. They are a most agreeable relief against the tangled mazes and constant jars of ordinary life, and the wide separations and contrasts of peoples and nations. And the poet laureate of England, has well voiced the sentiments of our age in his anticipations of the period when

> The war drum throbs no longer and the battle-flags are furled
> In the Parliament of man, the Federation of the world.

And in his loud call,—

> Forward, forward, let us range.
> Let the great world spin forever down the ringing grooves of change:
> Through the shadow of the globe, we sweep into the younger day.

Such an anticipation as this is so familiar as

to have become one of the commonplaces of human thought. All men look forward to that

> One far-off divine event,
> To which the whole creation moves.

But it was another matter three thousand years ago. Then neither the reasonings of philosophers, nor the plans of statesmen, nor the dreams of poets took in so wide a range. They knew of kingdoms, and tribes, and races; but of the human race as a whole, as bound together by a common origin, a common nature, and a common destiny—of this they had not the remotest conception. It was left for a band of singers in small, obscure, despised Palestine to anticipate a reign of righteousness, which should unite all the children of men under one sceptre. And they set it forth not merely as a possible or desirable event, but as one certain to occur; and they did this not simply in some favored moment of prophetic inspiration, but again and again—not only in one particular connection, but in a great variety of relations. The fact seems to have entered into the habitual current of their devout meditations, and they declare it in tones of the most absolute conviction and certainty. And when men now undertake to describe "the good time coming," they can find no better materials for their purpose than those furnished by the old Hebrew poets. The question recurs—What was it that lifted these men so greatly above all their contemporaries, and gave them such prescience of the far-distant future? How did their thoughts come to take this direction, when there was nothing in their situation or surroundings to suggest it? The only possible answer is found in the statement that they sang under a divine impulse. It is vain to remind us that the poet is a seer—that a sublime and fiery genius enables its possessor to see what escapes the notice of ordinary men. No genius was equal to a task like this. The Hebrews had in their immediate neighborhood a crowd of minor kingdoms, all idolatrous, debased, and sensual. On the south lay Egypt with its massive temples, its stately ritual, its profound symbolism, and as bent upon its idols as it was in the days of Abraham. On the east were the great military empires upon the Tigris and Euphrates, which indeed changed from time to time as a new tribe or family came in the ascendant, but never showed any amelioration in faith or in morals. What uplifting of mere human faculties could enable a

Jew to foresee that all this imperial magnificence would pass entirely away, and its elaborate and gorgeous idolatries utterly disappear, and that not only the people of these proud and ancient kingdoms, but all others, should become willing servants of the One True God? The question answers itself.

The same thing may be said of the teaching as to the individual man—How came these singers of a comparatively unlettered race, widely separated from the intellectual life of the rest of mankind, and without the stimulus of great schools and philosophies, to describe so accurately man's glory and his shame? Without elation they set forth his origin as the creature of God, the child of God, and little less than divine, superior to all else that the earth contains, and finding his truest honor and blessedness in communion with his infinite Maker. On the other hand, in their tremendous impeachment of human nature as fallen, we see not a trace of satire or cynicism. They say harder things than are found in Juvenal or Horace, or any of their imitators, but there is nothing that looks like misanthropy. Their intense earnestness is blended and balanced with a tenderness and compassion which forbid every malign emotion. With the fall they see the possibility of restoration, and for this all needful provision is made in the disclosure of Jehovah's wonderful condescension and loving-kindness.

This, then, is the trinity of truths respecting the race which are taught by the Psalter, with a precision, variety, fulness, and force, not surpassed even by the New Testament. First, man's original position as a son of God by creation, stamped with his Maker's image, and endowed with His dominion over the animal world, but himself governed only by reason and conscience. Secondly, his subsequent fall from that high estate, so as to become the prey of sin and guilt, feeding on ashes, out of harmony with his God and with himself, a blind Samson groping amid the ruins of his original home, and pursued by the spectres of remorse and fear. Thirdly, the prodigal coming back from his long wandering, acknowledging with shame and blinding tears his sinful errors, caught up in a father's arms, restored to his old place in that father's heart, then through his fellowship with heaven, renewing his fellowship with earth, and seeing in all the countless tribes of the world his fellow-subjects of the Supreme Will, and his destined fellow-partakers in the riches of the Divine Mercy. These truths no other set of men even thought out, much less made them their own by such a living experience that they were uttered in poetry and song with pathos, with fiery energy, with sublime glory, with more than earthly beauty. Not one discordant note is heard in the whole collection. The reason, the only reason is that along with the poetic inspiration in these sweet singers of Israel, there was the afflatus of the Divine Spirit, and the Psalter came from God.

# LECTURE IV.

THE MESSIAH AND A FUTURE LIFE.

# LECTURE IV.

### THE MESSIAH AND A FUTURE LIFE.

THE DOCTRINE OF A MESSIAH PECULIAR TO THE OLD TESTAMENT—HOW IT IS STATED IN THE PSALTER—THE SECOND PSALM—THE FORTY-FIFTH—THE SEVENTY-SECOND—THE ONE HUNDRED AND TENTH—THE TWENTY-SECOND—THE CHARACTER THUS DESCRIBED—UNLIKE THE HINDU AVATARA—THE PERSIAN SOSIOSH—NOT OF SUBJECTIVE ORIGIN—DOCTRINE OF A FUTURE LIFE—OF LITTLE VALUE *per se*—KNOWN TO THE PSALMISTS—NOT DWELT UPON—HOW ITS PLACE WAS SUPPLIED—THE ARGUMENT SUMMED UP.

THE fallen condition of man is not only a doctrine of Scripture, but a fact of universal experience and observation. All the religions of the heathen world bear witness to this fact, and to their own incompetency to deal with it. They could devise no effectual relief. Mankind yearned for that which it could not find, which in itself it did not possess. Neither mythology nor philosophy could give any assurance of redemption. Men cried aloud to heaven, but they received no answer. The attempts even of the wisest and best, whether among Aryan or Semitic races, are not unfitly represented in the words of a living poet,—

> An infant crying in the night;
> An infant crying for the light;
> And with no language but a cry.

It may be said, therefore, with truth, that the doctrine of the MESSIAH, at least in any clearly developed form, is peculiar to the Old Testament. There are indeed scattered through the Pagan mythologies obscure allusions to a future deliverer, but nowhere is there anything to show that this conception held the place which it occupied among the Hebrews, lying as it did at the very basis of their national existence, and giving shape and color to all their institutions. The first promise was uttered at the gates of Paradise; it was renewed to Noah, the second father of the race; it was the reason of the call of Abraham from Chaldea to Canaan; it was perpetuated in his family; it underlay the institution of the priestly and prophetic orders in the Mosaic Cultus; and finally it blossomed out in the monarchy established in the line of David. That is, by the time of this eminent man, the history of the chosen people had been so developed, its ecclesiastical and political constitution had become so fixed, and the cycle of its fortunes had been so diversified, that abundant material was furnished for expanding and illustrating the Messianic Conception in every appropriate way. Accordingly, in the great era of lyric poetry which began with David, we should naturally expect to find this lofty national hope set forth. And so it is. There are no songs in praise of the national heroes, a negative fact still more markedly exhibited in the hymn of Moses at the Red Sea, and that of Deborah upon the overthrow of Sisera. In neither is there any lauding of the human instruments of the triumph, but the entire glory is given to Israel's God. So the Psalter contains not a single pæan in honor of any one illustrious personage of earthly origin, from Abel and Enoch down to David and his mighty men.

But it does contain a number of Psalms which celebrate in a peculiar and otherwise unexampled method the sufferings and the glories of one extraordinary personage. And they do this in such a way as to make it apparent that they are a fair expression of the national thought. They present to us predictions of the great future deliverer, not abstractly nor historically, not as belonging entirely to remote ages, but as a living hope in the present and as developed out of the existing experience of God's people. The hopes and fears, the trials and triumphs, the temptations and confessions and prayers and praises of believers, flowering into song and uttering themselves in that poetic form which always seems most appropriate to deep emotion —it would indeed be strange, if these lyrics contained no reference to that which always was the ground-idea of the nation's existence. Nor is it wonderful that there are Psalms in which at first it is difficult to determine to what extent and according to what law they are pervaded by the Messianic element. The prophets, priests, and kings of the Old Testament were adumbrations of One who should comprehend in His own person all these offices. The nation itself was indissolubly connected with its future head, and on that account shared and anticipated his fortunes. Hence there are so many instances in which language is used respecting the type which belongs only to the antitype, and others in which the singer almost insensibly passes from utterances appropriate only to himself or the people he represents, to utterances which necessarily suggest the thought of some one spotless, if not divine, with whom the people stand in intimate and mysterious union. But in all cases the drapery of the Psalms is native and national. There are no exotics in the garden of the Hebrew muse. The imagery is taken from the circumstances of the time and place; and the poet expresses himself according to his training and experience. Hence the seemingly fragmentary character of the Messianic Psalms. No one of them gives a view of Messiah's whole person or work or character, but each one takes that portion or feature which needed at the time to be set forth, leaving it for future ages or the progress of events to adjust these separate statements into one harmonious and self-consistent portraiture. To quarrel with this arrangement is to quarrel with the entire system of lyric poetry, or with its use as a mode of Divine revelation.

What, now, is the Messiah of the Psalms? I propose to answer this question by citing in succession some of the lyrics, which by immemorial tradition, and by the almost concurrent voice of scholars of our own day, are admitted to refer chiefly, if not exclusively, to Christ. Let me begin with the Second, the most finish-ed and striking poem in the entire collection. Indeed I know of none in any language that surpasses it in regularity of structure and depth of poetic feeling. It consists of four strophes of equal length, each containing a distinct portion of the theme. In the first the poet hears the tramp of gathering armies, and as the tumultuous host draws near, sees whole nations in revolt and recognizes the presumptuous words of their leaders. And so he breaks out in a question of wonder and horror, " Why do nations rage, and peoples imagine a vain thing? Kings of the earth have set themselves, and princes have taken counsel against Jehovah and His anointed, saying, Let us break their bonds asunder, and cast their cords from us." Then all at once, in the second strophe, he lifts his eye far away from this tempest of confusion, and sees Jehovah seated upon His everlasting throne, mocking at the fatuity of His adversaries, and calmly announcing, to their terror and confusion, that He had set His king upon His holy hill. Then in the third strophe, by a sudden and most dramatic change of speakers, the anointed king comes in, affirming, on the authority of Jehovah, his own Divine Sonship, the grant to him of a strictly universal dominion, and of power to exercise that dominion, whether in wrath or in mercy. Lastly, in the fourth strophe, the poet summons kings and judges to desist from their hopeless enterprise, and kissing the Son to experience the blessedness of all who take refuge in Him. It seems to be plain that the person here described could not possibly be David or any of his line. The boundaries of the promised land had been definitely fixed by the Divine Word, and were never exceeded in fact; but here is a covenant that Jehovah's anointed Son should have and exercise an unlimited dominion, on the ground of which earthly rulers indiscriminately are advised to yield Him implicit obedience.

In the Forty-fifth Psalm, this mighty ruler reappears. He is girded with a sword. He rides forth prosperously. His arrows are sharp, and peoples fall under Him. But the poet celebrates with emphasis the moral groundwork of this dominion. The Conqueror is beautiful beyond all human standard or comparison, *i. e.*, invested with every moral and spiritual attraction. Grace is poured into His lips. He loves righteousness and hates iniquity. For this reason God anoints Him and blesses Him forever. Nay, He is even addressed as divine—" Thy throne, O

God, is forever and ever." But this King has a bride richly dressed in gold inwoven garments, who, loaded with gifts and followed by virgins, enters with music and song into the palace, where the dynasty thus established is to have perpetual succession and endless fame. Here is a plain reference to the familiar figure used all through the sacred Scriptures, by which the relation between God and His people, and so between Christ and His Church, is represented as a conjugal tie. To consider the Psalm as a glowing epithalamium upon the marriage of a mere earthly monarch, is simply absurd. No king of the Hebrew, or of any other race, ever founded his title to his throne simply upon his moral qualities, his love of truth, meekness and righteousness. Yet this is preëminently the case here. Because the King is so upright, God bestows upon Him an eternal blessing, and nations give Him thanks forever.

The same point is somewhat differently elaborated in the Seventy-second Psalm. Here is described by Solomon a superhuman King whose empire far transcends his own. It reaches from sea to sea, and from the river to the ends of the earth, *i. e.*, from each frontier of the promised land to the remotest regions of the known world in the opposite quarter: from the Mediterranean to the ocean that washes the shores of Eastern Asia, and from the Euphrates to the utmost west. Before its ruler, all who are most inaccessible to the arms of Israel, hasten to tender their voluntary submission. The wild sons of the desert, the merchants of Tarshish, the islanders of the Mediterranean, the Arab chiefs, the wealthy Ethiopians, are foremost in proffering their homage and fealty. But this is not enough. All kings are to fall down before Him—all nations are to do Him service. His empire is to be coextensive with the world, and is to last while the moon endures. He Himself may be out of sight, but His Name will endure forever—that name will propagate itself as long as the sun shines, and men shall be blessed in Him to the end of time. Yet this kingdom is spiritual; it confers peace upon the world only by righteousness. Its Head has profound sympathy with the poor and the helpless. He hears the cry of every human heart; He brings relief to every human sufferer. So that His appearance is like the rain upon the mown grass, like showers that water the earth. He is formidable only to oppressors, whom He breaks in pieces; but the needy, the afflicted, and the friendless, are the objects of His peculiar care. And it is upon this fact, upon the equity and grace of the King, that the universality and perpetuity of His kingdom are founded.

Yet again, we meet with this lofty personage in the One Hundred and Tenth Psalm. Here He is introduced at once, as sitting on the right hand of Jehovah, as the partner of His dignity and power. Exalted thus, He has enemies, but they are doomed to a remediless overthrow. Nations and kings and the wide earth shall feel the resistless rod of His strength. When He musters His host, His people willingly offer themselves for the service, clad not in earthly armor, but in the beauties of holiness. And they come in countless multitude and never-ending succession, like dewdrops from the womb of the morning. But their ruler is Priest as well as King;—not Levitical, nor Aaronic, but of that older order, which in the person of the mysterious Melchizedek had been honored even by the Father of the faithful. According to this lofty type, the Messiah has neither beginning of days nor end of life, but sits forever a priest upon His throne. And He is Priest-king manifestly in order that some work of expiation may be accomplished by which His people shall become prepared to offer themselves willingly to His service, and thus be worthy of sharing in His universal conquests. In this double capacity, uniting the two functions, regal and sacerdotal, which to the Jewish mind always stood separate and distinct, the consecrated Monarch sets forth against His foes. When wearied in the pursuit, like Gideon's warriors He refreshes Himself with water from the brook, and marches on, conquering and to conquer.

But the image of the Priest suggesting as it does the thought of sacrifice, reminds us of another order of ideas respecting the Messiah which might naturally be expected to occur in the Psalms. Accordingly from these bright and glowing pictures of regal majesty and power and victory, I turn back toward the beginning of the collection, where we find quite a new conception of the entire subject. It is in the Twenty-second Psalm, the song upon Aijeleth Shahar, the hind of the morning, a title in which it is with some probability supposed that the *hind* is a poetical figure for persecuted innocence, and the *morning* (literally, *dawn*) for deliverance after long distress. The lyric concludes with a graphic picture of the same universal prevalence of truth and right already presented, but comes to it in a very different way. The clash of arms is not heard once, nor the blare of trumpets. The opening words are the cry of a sufferer pleading for help. Apparently abandoned by heaven and earth, He is in the last extremity. Furious enemies assail Him on every side, while He Himself is wasted away, His body reduced to a skeleton, His hands and His feet pierced; and as He is thus hovering on the brink of death, His foes feast their eyes on the spectacle and cast lots over His raiment. But just here His loud cry for help passes into a confident anticipation of deliverance. The consequences of this deliverance will be universal and everlasting. The rescued sufferer will thank and praise God among all the seed of Israel, so that their heart shall live forever. Not only so, but He will perform His vows by suitable offerings and sacrifices, and to the joyful eucharistic table thus spread shall come not only His brethren, but all kindreds of the nations from one end of the earth to the other. The rich and the poor alike shall gather to the festive assembly. Nor shall the celebration cease with the contemporary race, but go down from age to age to generations yet unborn. For the Kingdom is the

Lord's, and He is Governor among the nations.

Such is the substance of five Messianic Psalms. There is a score or more besides, the recital of which would add to the liveliness and the fulness of the delineation, but there is not time to cite them. For the same reason I have not entered upon nice questions of exegesis, nor attempted to explain or defend the principles upon which the utterance of these far-reaching predictions is reconciled with the character and condition of their respective authors. Nor is it any part of the plan to found an argument upon the fulfilment of prophecy as shown by the correspondence between many of the detailed expressions of the Psalter, and the recorded life and death and resurrection of our blessed Lord. This is an interesting and fruitful theme, but it does not belong here. All that concerns the present argument is simply the existence of these remarkable poems in a popular lyric collection of the Hebrew people, largely and constantly used in their social and public worship. I have analyzed their contents and briefly stated their general meaning, as it is ascertained by the fixed laws of language. Nor does this statement rest simply upon the authority of the

New Testament. Had that book never been written, these Psalms would necessarily have the same meaning as has been attributed to them. The question, then, recurs, how are we to account for such a peculiar phenomenon in literature? We are dealing, not with prose, but with poetry; not with a stately epic, but with verses intended to be sung. We are brought into contact with the throbbing heart of a people giving free utterance to all its hopes and fears, its recollections and its anticipations, in its relations to God. Here is a distinct class of sacred odes, which, leaving aside both the past and the present, distinctly points to the future, and declares the coming of One who is to introduce the reign of universal truth and peace. While He is invested with irresistible might, and wields an iron sceptre, yet He is Himself personally an example of rectitude and truth and grace, and the whole force of His administration turns in this direction. He overthrows the proud and the wicked, but is a shelter to all the humble poor. He starts from the holy hill of Zion; He is a product of the Jewish race; He is to sit upon David's throne; but His blessings—not simply His authority, but the benefits He confers—are to be felt to the end of the earth. He is, too, not only a king, but a priest, and in some undefined way His sufferings are connected with His triumph; so that the former are the cause of the latter. Of course, in our day, we understand the exact nature of this connection, for we have the words of Him who expounded the things written of Him in the Law of Moses, and in the Prophets, and in the Psalms (Luke xxiv. 44), and who said to the two disciples on the way to Emmaus—"Ought not Christ to have suffered these things, and to enter into His glory?" (xxiv. 26). The contemporaries of David had no such illumination, but they had the record, from which they could scarcely fail to infer that moral causes lay at the foundation of the Messianic Empire, and that humiliation must precede exaltation. Whence, then, did this conception originate? It was not an importation from any other race or faith, for no other had it. The last hundred years have thrown a flood of light upon all the literature and traditions of the ancient nations of Eastern and Central Asia. Neither Egyptians, nor Brahmans, nor Buddhists, nor Confucianists, nor Parsees, nor Accads, nor Chaldeans, ever formed a conception of a future deliverer approaching the Hebrew notion, in distinctness, in purity, in tenderness, in universality. Their views were distorted by mythological legends or absurd fancies. Compare the Hindu *Avatára* as given in the Sanscrit Scriptures. Vishna is represented as coming into the world in ten, some say twenty-four, successive transformations, for the purpose of redressing wrong and preserving the creation. These consist of a series of hideous physical generations in the shape of a fish, a tortoise, a boar, a lion, a dwarf, etc., in all of which metamorphoses there is a boundless store of legendary words and deeds, but all of them destitute of any spiritual meaning or moral purpose. What resemblance is there between these grotesque and often immoral developments, and the picture of a wise, and just, and benignant, and glorious king, formidable only to the wicked, and at last gathering high and low, rich and poor, under one peaceful sceptre? There is, indeed, some resemblance in the *Sosiosh* of the Avestan—the expected deliverer of the Perso-Aryan race, who, when evil had reached its final stage, was to appear, and by a process of resurrection and judgment, destroy at last all the wicked, purge out the dross from created nature, and gather the whole race of man on a new-born earth to sing the glory of Ormazd and the Amshaspands. But this part of the Zendic Scriptures belongs, if not to post-Christian, certainly to a very late period in the development of Zoroaster's doctrine, and therefore is generally and justly supposed to have been a reproduction of views borrowed from the Jews, whose writings we know were widely disseminated all through the East after the first overthrow of Babylon. Where, then, did the Jews get the brilliant conception of a Messiah, so inwrought into the literature and the life of the people, that it rang constantly in the choruses of the temple, and was the sheet-anchor of the nation in every time of trial—the pivot of their firmest hopes, and the key to all their Scriptures? Modern writers make its origin human and subjective. They say it was the joint product of the misfortunes of the times and the theocratic constitution—the experience of a felt want in this and other instances exciting the imagination to fill up the blank out of its own resources. But how can this theory, however ingeniously wrought out, explain the Psalms we have been considering? These are all of the Davidic or Solomonic period, when the nation was united under one head, in a state of great prosperity, and with boundaries equalling the widest range ever mentioned in the original grant of Canaan. What subjective considerations could have led writers in that age, when even the idea of a universal history was unknown, to conceive of a monarch who, by divine appointment, should go forth from Zion and rule literally all the earth, who should do this in the strictest exercise of righteousness, and should introduce a peaceful state of general prosperity, and yet combining priestly with kingly functions, should in some way suffer the extremest sorrow as the prelude of His signal and eternal triumph? No known laws of human nature will account for such a result, and no similar case can be furnished from all the records of human experience. It follows, therefore, that these Psalms were divinely suggested.

From the Messiah I pass to the doctrine of a FUTURE LIFE in the Psalms. The absence of full and explicit reference to this subject has not unfrequently been a source of perplexity, even to believers. If the Psalter is the one divinely appointed Liturgy of the Church in all ages; if its fervent ritual of devotion was intended to revolve within the circle of every-day pains, fears, and solaces of our earthly pilgrimage, and furnish the fittest material for prayer, praise, trust, and hope, why is there so little reference to the final outcome of our present life, to the better world beyond the grave? In answer to this question it may be observed:

(1). That the doctrine of Immortality (*per se*) is far from deserving the emphasis which has been placed upon it. It is very true that the absence of the belief is a serious reproach. One can hardly sufficiently reprobate the crude materialism which at the present day, and often under the pretence of relying upon the results of scientific investigation, coolly dismisses all thought of a life to come as a mere dream, pleasing indeed, and affording an agreeable excitement to the imagination, but utterly destitute of any rational basis. Far better is the stout assertion of Max Müller, that " the *sine qua non* of all real religion, is a belief in immortality and in personal immortality, without which religion is like an arch resting upon one pillar—like a bridge ending in an abyss." Whoso holds that man, when the breath leaves the body, perishes like the beasts, is in great danger of coming to act upon the beastly-maxim, " Let us eat and drink, for to-morrow we die." But it does not follow from this, that all who are persuaded that there is a future life are necessarily possessors of a pure, or elevated, or satisfying theology. There are numerous examples to the contrary, alike among nations of the highest refinement and among tribes of wandering savages. In ancient Egypt we have the best developed conception of man's immortality which any of the heathen attained—one that included the ethical ideas of judgment and retribution. Yet this did not save its holders from the grossest forms of polytheism. For they worshipped even brute animals—a custom which provoked the scorn not only of Christians, but of the heathen. The words of Clement of Alexandria are familiar; speaking of a visitor's disappointment when passing through the long and stately propylons and halls of a magnificent temple gleaming with jewels and gold, till he reached at last the most holy recess, a veil was drawn aside and revealed the god, in the shape of a bull, or a cat, or a crocodile, or a serpent! Plutarch before him reprobated this animal-worship as a fit subject of laughter and ridicule. Among the Fijians of the South Sea, the belief of immortality led to the most revolting bloodshed; for arguing that man's state after death will be precisely that in which he was when he died, they destroyed their parents, and sometimes themselves, while in full health and strength, in the hope of thus escaping here and hereafter the evils of age and decrepitude. And Livingstone mentions numerous tribes of Central Africa who, when a chief dies, slaughter a number of his slaves to be his companions in the other world. So the wild tribes of North America all held firmly that there was a future life, but almost the only result was to intensify the gloom and terror which belong to all natural religions. It is clear, then, that there is no religious character and no ethical importance in this much-lauded tenet. All depends upon the other doctrines with which it is associated.

(2). That it was known and held by the authors of the Psalms is very evident. Their fathers must have learned it during their long stay in Egypt, where it was represented in painting, in architecture, and in literature. Besides, they must have inferred it from man's original creation in the image of God; from the translation of Enoch, and from Jehovah's persistent application to Himself of the title—the God of Abraham, and the God of Isaac, and the God of

Jacob, long after those patriarchs had ceased to live on the earth. Nay, the very superstitions of the people bear witness on this point. We find that from the time of Moses there was constantly a class of persons who professed to be mediums of communication between this world and the other. They were called *Necromancers*, or *Seekers to the dead*—(Deut. xviii. 11, Isaiah viii. 19). See the case of Saul and the witch of Endor. It does not make any difference whether we call this practice a delusion or an imposture. In either case, its prevalence and long continuance show that the popular Jewish mind was deeply pervaded by a conviction that the soul existed after this life. But since the vulgar held this truth without living reference to God, they only made it a miserable superstition. But besides, there are utterances in the Psalms themselves which imply the conviction that there is a life beyond the present. In the Sixteenth, the sacred poet, looking death full in the face, said:

> Thou wilt not abandon my soul to the unseen world,
> Nor suffer Thy holy one to see the pit.
> Thou wilt show me the path of life,
> Fulness of joy in Thy presence,
> Pleasures at Thy right hand forevermore.

So again in the Seventeenth, contrasting himself with men of the world who have their portion in this life, who are sated with children to whom they bequeath their wealth, the poet says:

> As for me, in righteousness I shall behold Thy face,
> I shall be satisfied, when I awake, with Thy likeness;

— a jubilant hope which never could have been bounded by the grave. A similar contrast is found in the Forty-ninth Psalm, where the singer describes the vanity of men, even in their best estate. Although rich, and honored, and wise, they have no permanence. They perish like cattle; they are laid in the grave; Death is their shepherd; their beauty and their glory are gone. But he adds, "God shall redeem my soul from the power of the grave, for He shall take me." He who knows and loves God, has the life of God, and can never utterly perish. That bond must survive even the shock of death. To the same effect, and partly in the same words, is the utterance of Asaph in the Seventy-third Psalm. In this striking lyric, the writer, after solving the painful mystery of prosperous ungodliness, declares that as for himself, he is ever held by God's hand, and therefore has unshaken confidence. "Thou wilt guide me with Thy counsel, and afterward receive me to glory. My flesh and my heart faileth, but God is the strength of my heart and my portion forever." Now it is true that there are other utterances differing very widely from these, such as the following:

In death there is no remembrance of Thee,
In the grave who shall give Thee thanks?—(vi. 5).

What profit is there in my blood when I go down to the pit?
Shall the dust praise Thee? Shall it declare Thy truth?—(xxx. 9)

Wilt Thou show wonders unto the dead?
Shall the shades below arise and give Thee thanks?
Shall Thy loving-kindness be told in the grave?
Or thy faithfulness in destruction?—(lxxxviii. 10, 11).

These sorrowful forebodings were uttered under a sense of desertion. Their authors felt themselves going down to death under a cloud, and considered their situation a token of the Divine displeasure. Their hopeless gloom arose not from the mere cessation of life, but from its cessation under the frown of the Almighty. If He were alienated from them, what hope had they here or hereafter? Hence these wailings of seeming despair!

(3). Still it is very evident that there is a sharp contrast between the teachings of the Old Testament and those of the New on the subject of immortality. In the latter there is a fulness, and confidence, and glow, and splendor which leave nothing to be desired. In the former the statements are scanty, infrequent, and sometimes apparently at least ambiguous. And it is very certain that in the Psalter, which represents in the best way the practical side of dogma, there is no such reference to the truth as we should expect. Why is this? Why do these devout singers say so much less of the future life than their heathen contemporaries? Why is there not even an allusion to the process of judgment upon every disembodied spirit in the Hall of Osiris, which their forefathers must have seen or heard of during their long stay in the Nile valley? In short, why is there the possession of the truth, and yet so little use of it? The answer to these questions furnishes the argument I offer in the case. The reticence of the Psalmists was divinely ordered. The dispensation to which they belonged was an inchoate one. It was to bridge over the interval between the fall of man and the fulness of time for the appearance of the great Revealer of God. For that Revealer was to make the full disclosure of God's purposes of love and mercy toward His people. By His coming He " abolished death and brought life and immortality to light." This was not simply the truth that death is not the end of man. That was known, or at least believed, the world over and among all races. But the New Testament sets forth *life and immortality* in the highest sense—comprehending the resurrection of the body in a new and glorious form; its reunion with the soul; perfect freedom from all the stain and power of sin; the vision of God, and the endless and ever-increasing enjoyment of His favor. Now these things could not be fairly conceived and satisfactorily applied until the actual manifestation of the Son of God. In His life, and death, and rising again from the dead, and His ascension on high, there was furnished the proper historical basis for an intelligent and satisfying faith on these points. And it was proper that for Him whom God sent last of all, it should be reserved fully to lift the veil of the future and disclose what the Lord has prepared for them that love Him. Hence the sparing references to these themes in the Psalms. The reserve was not accidental, but designed; not the result of ignorance, but of knowledge. Had the Psalmists been left to themselves they would have done like the rest of mankind—joked about Charon and his boat, or constructed an elaborate "Ritual of the Dead," like the Egyptians, or adopted some form of the Hindu transmigration of souls, or anticipated the sensual paradise of Moslems, the warrior banquets of Scandinavians, or the happy hunting-grounds of our own Aborigines. But they did nothing of the kind. Their references to the subject are always connected with the idea of God. If of a hopeful character, they anticipate being in happy union with Him; if of a desponding purport, the great sorrow is that the chorus of His praise must cease. Everything revolves around the one central thought of the Supreme, holy, and ever-blessed God, as the abiding and all-sufficient source of their happiness.

Here, then, lies the peculiar, and, on natural principles, inexplicable position of the Psalmists. Having the living roots of the doctrine in their earlier literature, and meeting with varied forms of it among the heathen with whom they came in contact, they yet habitually and carefully refrained from any prolonged or minute references to it. The fruitfulness and attractiveness of the theme is apparent in all literature; not only in that of the ethnic religions, but also and eminently in that of Christendom, from the splendid imagery of the Apocalypse, down through the hymnology of all ages and lands, even to our own date. Upon scarce any theme does the Christian poet rise on loftier wing, or take a wider sweep of imaginative conception, than when expatiating upon the future glories of the believer. But the old Psalmists stay their hands. They delight to dwell on the Divine perfections or the glory of the Divine government. They are never weary of setting forth the trust and confidence and peace and joy that are found in fellowship with the unseen Jehovah. This is represented in the largest variety of phrase:— the shadow of a great rock in a weary land, manna in the wilderness, gushing streams in the desert, the dawn of morning to a weary night-watcher, a shelter from the storm, a portion sweeter than honey, more desirable than gold. But as soon as they approach the life to come, they give but a glance within the veil, and then retreat to dwell upon the present spiritual relations of the creature and his Creator. For here was all that was needed. If the Almighty reveals Himself in condescension and love to His people as their God—their dwelling place, the rock of their strength—this involves an endless relation, for surely the living God would not expend His riches of love upon perishing creatures of clay whose houses are crushed before the moth. We see and feel this as a matter of course. And to us a mere naked immortality, such as is found among the lowest tribes of men, bears no comparison in dignity and value to the idea of a present happy life with God. But the marvel is, that the Hebrew singers understood this so distinctly, and were controlled by it so entirely in their most impassioned utterances.

The case, then, stands thus: On the one side we find the doctrine of the soul's immortality holding a fixed and prominent place among the articles of popular belief the world over, in ancient times as well as modern. This position has been indeed at times attacked, but never successfully. The evidence adduced from the old Sanscrit texts, or the graven or painted walls of Thebes or Philae, or the cuneiform inscriptions of Nineveh or Persepolis, or the literature of Greece and Rome, or the consensus of modern travelers, is altogether too abundant and clear to be resisted. The belief was so widespread, if not universal, as to compel us to attribute it to the common instincts of man's nature. As Coleridge says, " Its fibres are to be traced to the tap-root of humanity." But the belief was always expressed in gross and inadequate forms, and associated with outlandish views, as if to show that our fallen nature, left to itself, could not frame any rational view of the mode of existence in the world to come, or of the character of its retributions. Hence men devised the fables of Elysium and Tartarus, the Metempsychosis from one fleshly form into another, the absorption into the divine unity, and the like. Hence, too, the folly of the Necromancy of our own day, the self-styled Spiritualism which for a generation has been rampant in this country. This crude imposture boasts much of its clear disclosure of a future life, and indeed has converted some materialists. But wherein has there been any gain to human knowledge or happiness or character? The history of the movement has only added another to the many illustrations already on record, of the moral impotence of the doctrine of immortality held in and for itself to elevate or purify. "The power of an endless life" (Hebrew vii. 16) is something transcendent and ineffable; but if it be separated from its kindred thought of the eternal God as the moral governor of the world and the satisfying portion of the soul, it at once degenerates into grotesque or monstrous or puerile conceptions, or else resolves itself into a mere prolongation of the present state of things without essential change, and therefore destitute of any restraining or uplifting influence. The mere continuance of being after death is rather a metaphysical dogma than a religious truth, and may coexist with the crudest and most unspiritual notions. The Esquimaux, the Papuan, the wildest savages in the forests of Central Africa, have no doubt that the spirits of their departed ancestors survive, but in no degree does this conviction raise them in the scale of thinking beings.

On the other side, we find the doctrine among the Hebrews held indeed, and occasionally illustrated in a remarkable manner, but still not thrust forward or made prominent, and yet all its essential ends gained in the fullest manner. The Hebrew poets talk of man's mortality in a strain of effectiveness and pathos nowhere surpassed. They represent the frailty, the vanity, the emptiness of human pursuits and expectations, with a keenness which no satirist of Greece or Rome has exceeded. And yet their doctrine of man's kinship with God, of his filial relation, of his capacities of holiness, of his faith in the unseen, of the superiority of spiritual things to temporal, of the certain overthrow of the transgressor and the equally certain recompense of the righteous, of the forgiveness of sin upon repentance and confession, and of the blessedness of the new life thus secured—this doctrine, I say, quite restored the scale, and put man in his social and religious relations in a position which no other ancient nation even approached. It is pertinent, then, again to ask, What occasioned this remarkable difference? How comes it to pass that in one nation—and that not distinguished by a philosophical spirit, nor by a gift for speculative inquiries—we find inwrought not only in its formal creed and national history, but also in its pious meditations and lyric songs, a marked and seemingly studied reticence upon the life beyond the grave, united with an intensely pure and spiritual conception of all divine things? The only answer is, that they were divinely guided. This superintendence on the one hand kept them from the vain and foolish imaginations which deluded all their contemporaries, and on the other refused to grant that degree of illumination which would have been inconsistent with the design and character of the inchoate system to which they belonged.

In conclusion, let me suggest the contrasted relations of the two themes we have been considering. Both refer to the Future, and yet how differently treated! Of the coming Messiah there is abundant mention—His person, His offices, His suffering, His kingdom, His glory, His moral excellence, His world-wide influence, His imperishable name. The picture is so complete, so vivid, so striking, that it requires a vigorous imagination to find any tolerable analogies to it in the literatures of other ancient nations. Yet in regard to Immortality, the contrast is the other way. Here the Hebrew singers are reticent and obscure. Occasionally a rift for a moment parts the clouds, and one catches a glimpse of the pleasures forevermore; but in an instant the curtain is drawn again, and it is the present relations of the soul to God that occupy all the attention. The ethnic religions, on the contrary, all habitually point forward to what follows this life, making indeed sad work of it. For just as the old map-makers filled the unexplored regions of Central Africa with figures of unicorns and elephants and all sorts of mythical wild beasts, so these peopled the unknown beyond with monstrous imaginations which terrified, but could not attract. Now it is on this departure from the beaten track of all the world that the argument bases itself. Why, in that outlook upon the future which all thoughtful men must take—and the more when the soul is roused by deep experiences—why do the Hebrew poets say so little of one theme on which others are profuse and animated, and yet linger long and lovingly on the theme upon which these others have little or nothing to say? The reason can not be found in race or soil or climate or national character or institutions or surroundings. The only sufficient and intelligible cause is given in the fact that the sacred singers of Palestine were under the control of a superior Power, which without impairing their freedom, yet guided their choice of themes, and the way in which they treated those themes.

# LECTURE V.

THE ETHICS OF THE PSALMS.

# LECTURE V.

### THE ETHICS OF THE PSALMS.

A FAIR TEST—NEGATIVE EXCELLENCE—PURITY OF THE MORALITY—FREEDOM FROM ASCETICISM, FORMALISM, HYPOCRISY—LOWLY, YET JOYFUL AND FREE—NOT SELF-RIGHTEOUS—THE IMPRECATIONS VINDICATED—LORD MACAULAY AND DR. DUFF—HISTORY OF THE PSALTER—TESTIMONIES TO ITS WORTH—CONCLUSION.

"BY their fruits ye shall know them," is a maxim of universal and absolute truth. It holds good in morals, in political economy, in statesmanship, just as much as in all natural processes. Good fruit the world over indicates a good tree, and evil fruit an evil tree; and so in all other relations. Plans and theories and projects may be apparently rational and judicious, but if on trial the results are bad, men almost instinctively reason back from effects to causes, and insist that the underlying principles must be unsound. But in no department of human thought and action is this so manifest as in all that pertains to religion. If a book, or a doctrine, or a practice, can be shown to lead to immorality, that fact at once puts an end to dispute or doubt. In the nature of things, *i. e.*, in the constitution of human society under the control of one supreme and infinite Being, truth must be in order to goodness, sound principles must lead to virtuous living.

From the beginning this doctrine has been used in Christian Apologetics. Indeed, Gibbon, in his well-known enumeration of the secondary causes of the rapid propagation of the Gospel in the first centuries of our era, expressly mentions the pure morals of the followers of the new faith as a powerful and widespread influence in its favor, as it certainly was—and the more so, as this fact was shown to be the result of the holy precept and example of the founder of the system. But many, while admitting this claim, have tried to break its force by disparaging the elder Scriptures. They compliment the New Testament at the expense of the Old. No judicious defender of the faith will accept such compliments. Not only the nature of the case, but the painful results of experience during the last century, show that both Testaments constitute integral and constituent parts of one book, nor can they be separated without violence and harm. The Hebrew Scriptures are to the Greek what the foundation is to a house; and to cut them off is to leave Christianity like an exquisitely-shaped and proportioned pyramid floating in the air. He who surrenders Moses and the Prophets must, in logical consistency, surrender Christ and the Apostles in like manner. Of course the two portions of the book are not identical—if they were, why should there be two? They have differences, but these differences spring out of the fact that the revelation is a gradual one, of which the earlier portions point to the later, while the later presuppose the earlier. There will, therefore, naturally be in the concluding part a fulness and maturity not to be expected in what goes before. Yet, substantially the doctrinal and moral teaching will be the same.

Is this the fact? To answer this question out of the Psalter is the aim of the present Lecture. Here one has the advantage of seeing the matter in the fairest light. For lyric poems are expressions of experience—songs of the heart. They contain views of truth and duty, not arranged and tabulated as in a code or treatise, but actually felt and uttered under the varying circumstances of outward providence or inward struggles. The singer looks out upon God, or the external world, or his fellows, or inwardly upon his own past or present; and then his soul is stirred within him, his heart boils over, and he bursts into song. Such utterances must be sincere. They are wrung out of a great pressure from within, and they bear the stamp of their origin. They register the moral status of the poet with unfailing accuracy. In looking at this status, the first impression concerns its negative character. One finds a total absence of the coarseness, frivolity, or downright immorality so offensively prominent in the hymns to the gods preserved in some other religions. The whole atmosphere is one of seriousness and purity. There are no tales of mischievous adventure, of cunning tricks, or of sensual indulgences as in the Homeric Hymns; nor is there any identifying of God and Nature as one and the same, whether in the attractive or the terrible manifestations of physical phenomena, nor a habitual supplication for mere outward gifts, such as health, children, fertile pastures, bounteous harvests, victory over foes, which constitute the staple of the prayers in the Rig-Veda. One will look in vain through the entire Psalter for any compromise of morality, any deification of natural powers, any representation or suggestion of true happiness as possible or desirable apart from the knowledge and service of a holy God. It is an entirely safe book to put into the hands of the young, the inexperienced, or the ignorant. They can learn nothing which they will need to unlearn, nothing to weaken the moral forces of the soul, or give an unhealthy direction to the imagination.

But to say this is to say little in comparison with the truth. The Psalter not only does not impair the principles of morals, but in every way confirms and establishes them. It makes for righteousness throughout. The key-note is given in the first Psalm, often considered a sort of preface to the whole. The theme is the Happy Man. Who is he? Where is he to be found? How is he to be described? Is he known or made by the possession of wealth, or place, or learning, or power, or any other form of worldly good? Nay. He is the one who walks not in the way of the ungodly, nor stands in the way of sinners, nor sits in the seat of the scornful; but his delight is in the law of the Lord, and in that law he meditates day and night. Such a man is like a tree planted beside living streams whose fruit does not fail, neither does its leaf wither; whereas a wicked man is like the dry and worthless chaff which the wind drives away.

Here is suggested what is one of the most marked and discriminating features of the Hebrew Ethics, viz., that they are deeply rooted in religion. In all false religions, ancient and modern, and in some corrupt forms of Christianity, the two things are widely separated. A man may be moral without being religious, and *vice versa*. Religion is a set of tenets and ritual practices which may be carefully observed and yet leave the outward secular life wholly unaffected. Morality, on the other hand, is the discharge of social duties without respect to divine authority, or the sanctions of Providence. The Psalter knows nothing of this most mischievous divorce between integrity of life and the eternal, spiritual truth upon which all uprightness must rest. It uniformly represents God as governor and ruler—the source, the standard, and the efficacious cause of all moral good. Justice, temperance, truth, meekness, and love have indeed intrinsic value; but they press upon the heart and conscience of these singers, because they are part of the express will of God. The servant of Jehovah, as such, must have and exercise these qualities. See this finely set forth in a Psalm (xv.) usually thought to have been composed on occasion of the removal of the Ark to Zion:

> Lord, who shall abide in Thy tabernacle?
> Who shall dwell in Thy holy hill?

The answer is not, He that is circumcised, that comes to the great yearly festivals, that shuns unclean food, or anything of the kind, but

> He that walketh uprightly, and worketh righteousness,
> And speaketh truth in his heart:
> Who backbiteth not with his tongue,
> Nor doeth evil to his neighbor,
> Nor taketh up a reproach against his friend;
> In whose eyes a vile person is contemned,
> But he honoreth them that fear the Lord;
> Who sweareth to his own hurt and changeth not.
> He that doeth these things shall never be moved.

Is there anywhere a brighter picture of stainless honor, of lofty integrity?—yet the whole inseparably linked with the presence and favor of God as its origin and sanction.

Yet with this elevated standard of ethical principle there is nothing overstrained or exaggerated. There is not the least tinge of asceticism; no punishing of the body for the sins of the soul; no denial of the sweet charities of domestic life; no rejection of civil or political relations as inherently sinful or unbecoming; no praise of celibacy, or solitude, or any other form of voluntary renunciation of what is in itself innocent—nothing whatever in common with self-torturing Brahmans, or Jewish Essenes, or scornful Stoics, or even Christian stylites or anchorets. On the contrary, there are domestic, household, social, and patriotic Psalms. These compare brotherly affection to the dews of Hermon, or the fragrant oil of the sanctuary; God's continual providence to favors sent in sleep; children at one time to the olive plants around the table, at another to arrows which fill the quiver of a hero; while the daughters are corner-pillars polished after the similitude of a palace.

The Psalmists praise God as the Father of the fatherless, the Judge of the widow, who sets the solitary in families, and makes the barren woman the joyful mother of children. They exult in Jerusalem as the city of God, the mountain of His holiness, the place where His honor dwelleth, and invoke peace within her walls and prosperity within her palaces. And of Mount Zion they declare that it is beautiful for situation, the joy of the whole earth, a place more excellent and glorious than all the mountains of prey; God Himself establishes it forever. The whole tone here is peaceful, domestic, and national in the best sense. The morality is not that of slaves, or of hermits, or of philosophers, or of devotees, but of men, women, and children, engaged in all the usual relations of human life, but elevating and transfiguring these by a constant sense of their common obligation as children of the heavenly King, as subjects of a holy and beneficent law.

The purity of the Hebrew ethics is the more remarkable when one considers the minute and complicated ritual of worship in which all the authors of the Psalms were trained. The whole round of sacred persons and places and times was prescribed according to the pattern shown to Moses on the mount. The custom of sacrifices or offerings, bloody or unbloody, found in all the ancient nations, was here developed with amazing fulness. Every day the morning and the evening sacrifice was kindled. On the weekly, monthly, yearly festivals, besides innumerable occasions of a private or personal nature, the blood of bulls and goats ran, the smoke of incense ascended, the steam of burning flesh filled the courts of the tabernacle. The cultus was stately and imposing in the highest degree. Nothing, therefore, was more natural than for the worshippers to fall into what in modern times is called the *opus operatum* theory, and to attribute an intrinsic and inherent efficacy to the gorgeous ceremonial in which they were habitually engaged. This was a common error among the heathen. They supposed, or at least are represented by the poets as supposing, that hecatombs of victims and costly libations brought their divinities under obligation to them, so that it would be ungrateful and wrong not to show favor to such earnest and self-sacrificing worshippers. Nor is there any reason to doubt that a similar degrading notion at times obtained among the Hebrews. But it never found expression among the Psalmists. Again and again do they repudiate it, especially in the great judicial process described in the Fiftieth Psalm. Here Jehovah, revealing Himself in fire and tempest as at Sinai, summons the people before Him, and in lofty irony reproves the stupidity which would deem mere outward oblations any gratification to Him.

> I will not reprove thee for thy sacrifices,
> Or for thy burnt-offerings continually before Me.
> I will take no bullock out of thy house,
> Nor he-goats from thy folds.
> For every beast of the forest is Mine,
> And the cattle upon a thousand hills.
> I know all the fowls of the mountains,
> And whatever moveth in the fields is with Me.
> If I were hungry I would not tell thee,
> For the world is Mine, and the fulness thereof.
> Will I eat the flesh of bulls,
> Or drink the blood of goats?

Do I need such things, or is it possible for Me to use them? Yet it is to be observed that in avoiding one error the writer does not run into the opposite. Because sacrifices have no intrinsic merit and can not feed the Deity, it does not follow that they are useless. On the contrary, they were both needed and commanded. Hence soon after the vigorous expostulation just recited, follows the precept—

> Sacrifice to God thanksgiving,
> And so pay thy vows to the Most High.

The animal victims were still to be offered, but as symbolical expressions of penitence, faith, and devout affection. Presented in this way they fulfilled their function, and the believer would find his worship accepted and blessed.

In the latter part of the same Psalm we have a similar testimony against another error common among the professors of every faith. This is hypocrisy, the substitution of words for deeds, the homage which vice pays to virtue.

> Unto the wicked God saith,
> What hast thou to do to declare My statutes
> And take My covenant into thy mouth?
> Whereas thou hatest instruction,
> And hast cast My words behind thee.

And then He proceeds to specify violations of three of the commandments, concluding with the solemn words,—

> These things hast thou done
> And I kept silence;
> Thou thoughtest I was just like thyself.
> I will reprove thee,
> And array (thy sins) before thine eyes.

The uniform doctrine of the Psalter is that God requires truth in the inward parts. Men may forget His character and attempt to impose upon Him by sounding professions, but the effort is vain. The mask will be stripped off from every hypocrite, and all secret iniquities be brought to light. They who would walk so as to please God must have clean hands and a pure heart. Otherwise they only flatter themselves in their own eyes until their iniquity is found to be hateful.

It is often supposed that the law was regarded by the Old Testament believers as a yoke of bondage which they submitted to as a disagreeable necessity, slavishly fearing its punishment and selfishly looking forward to its reward. The holy singers teach us better things. They indeed were deeply conscious of their feebleness and dependence. Hear the cry of the 19th Psalm:

> Who can discern his errors?
> Clear Thou me from hidden faults.
> Keep back Thy servant also from presumptuous sins;
> Let them not have dominion over me.
> Then shall I be perfect,
> And I shall be clean from much transgression.

To the same effect is the long alphabetical 119th Psalm, which a recent German critic charges with monotony and poverty of thought, but in so doing only shows his own poverty of spiritual apprehension. In every age this singular lyric has been a chosen portion of Scripture to the spiritually-minded. Never wearied by its repetitions, or its apparent redundancies, they have found in each verse a new stimulus to pious meditation or fresh nutriment of devout feeling. The Psalm is a continued series of aphorisms expressing in every variety of phrase, on one hand the excellence of the divine law, and on the other the difficulty and yet the blessedness of conforming to it. Hence it is full of devout and earnest breathings after Jehovah's grace and help.

> Oh that my ways were directed to keep Thy statutes.
>
> My soul cleaveth to the dust;
> Quicken Thou me according to Thy word.
>
> Hold Thou me up, and I shall be safe.
>
> Order my footsteps in Thy word,
> And let not any iniquity have dominion over me.

The deep insight of these holy men into the radical corruption of human nature made them thoroughly sensible of the fact that good thoughts and good works have their source only in God. Yet while all this is true; while they, like the Apostle, found a law that when they would do good, evil was present with them, they also could and did say with the same Apostle, "I delight in the law of God after the inward man." Indeed we have an almost identical utterance in the 40th Psalm:

> To do Thy will, O my God, I delight,
> Yea, Thy law is within my heart.

That law to them was a badge, not of slavery, but of liberty. It gave light to the mind, it quickened the soul, it rejoiced the heart. The statutes of the Lord were more to be desired than gold, yea, than much fine gold, sweeter also than honey and the droppings of the comb.

> Oh, how I love Thy law!
> It is my meditation all the day.
>
> Seven times a day do I praise Thee,
> Because of Thy righteous judgments.

It is not necessary to affirm that these utterances express the feelings of all the people, or even the habitual state of those from whose lips they fell. It is enough if they are regarded as the product of some favored hours of devotion, for even then they stand as the norm of godly character, the standard which every one is to set before him. And they show what a moral elevation was reached by obscure singers in an obscure country, far, far away from the æsthetic completeness of Greece, yet kindling a fire of love to God and holy things at which every succeeding generation has been glad to light its torch.

But there are two objections to the ethical correctness of the Psalter which require notice. One of these rests upon the assertion not unfrequently made by the Psalmist of his integrity. I will quote one case as strong as any, that which is found in Psalm xviii. 20–24:

> The Lord rewarded me according to my righteouness;
> According to the cleanness of my hands hath He recompensed me.
> For I have kept the ways of the Lord,
> And have not wickedly departed from my God.
> I was also upright before Him,
> And kept myself from my iniquity.
> Therefore the Lord recompensed me according to my righteousness,
> According to the cleanness of my hands in His sight.

Such utterances are charged as breathing the very spirit of self-righteousness and irreligious pride, and as, therefore, wholly unworthy of sincere and candid persons, much more of the devout and God-fearing. But this is a great mistake. In all these passages the worshipper is not laying claim to a perfect holiness, for one and all agree in the petition (cxliii. 2),—

> Enter not into judgment with Thy servant,
> For in Thy sight no man living is righteous.

The consciousness of human guilt lay too deep for that. The explanation of the claim to righteousness is not found (as Hengstenberg holds) in the fact of an upright moral striving, a sincere bent of mind earnestly reaching after the fulfilment of the divine law, in view of which God may be expected to pardon many weaknesses. How such a view is to be reconciled with the doctrine of gratuitous justification I can not conceive. Far better is the ground that the Psalmist is speaking of the case as it stood between him and his enemies, and in that view meant his words to be taken in their literal sense. Consider, *e.g.*, his conflict with Saul. In this the right was all on one side. Toward the king, David's whole course was absolutely faultless. Hunted for his life, and persecuted in every possible way, he refused to retaliate even when it was in his power. He could, therefore, justly claim as against such opposers absolute rectitude. Such a protestation is quite consistent with a deep sense of sin before God. Thus Paul asserted that in his flesh there dwelt no good thing, and spoke of himself as the chief of sinners; yet when occasion required, he resolutely asserted his integrity, and made a long detail of his services and his sufferings (2 Corinthians xi. 21–31). And God is not displeased with even a heat of jealousy in His people when insisting upon their sincerity. And such declarations are useful to remind us of the necessity of being able, in the quarrel of the world with the Lord's people, evermore to insist that as to the things in which they assail us we are not assailable. It is not simply by passing feelings and vain imaginations that God's children are separated from others, but by a consistent outward life.

Another and far more formidable objection to the ethical excellence of the Psalms is based on the fearful imprecations which some of them contain. Among the most striking are the following:

Let them be confounded that seek after my soul;
Let them be turned back and brought to confusion that devise my hurt,
Let them be as chaff before the wind,
And let the angel of the Lord drive them.
Let their way be dark and slippery,
And let the angel of the Lord persecute them.—(xxxv. 4, 5, 6.)

Pour out Thy indignation upon them,
And let Thy wrathful anger take hold on them.
Add iniquity unto their iniquity,
And let them not come into Thy righteousness.—(lxix. 24, 27.)

Set Thou a wicked man over him,
And let Satan stand at his right hand.
When he is judged, let him be condemned;
And let his prayer become sin.

Let his children be fatherless,
And his wife a widow.—(cix. 6, 7, 9.)

O, daughter of Babylon, who art to be destroyed;
Happy shall he be that rendereth unto Thee
The deed which thou hast done to us.
Happy shall he be that taketh
And dasheth thy little ones against the rock.—(cxxxvii. 8, 9.)

Such terrible maledictions have often been a grief and perplexity to the Christian, and an occasion for cavil and scoffing to the sceptical. And although one can not go so far as to say with Mr. Froude, " Those who accept the 109th Psalm as the Word of God are far on their way toward *auto-da-fés* and massacres of St. Bartholomew," or to agree with Dean Stanley, who describes their spirit as " savage " (*Jewish Church*, II., 170); yet it must be confessed that at first at least there seems to be a sharp contrast to the mild and benignant tones of the New Testament. This has led some with Bishops Horne and Horsley to try to overcome the difficulty by rendering the verbs in the future tense, and so converting the imprecations into predictions. But I believe that this is now considered by all respectable scholars a mere evasion, and one that does violence to the settled laws of the Hebrew language. Besides, it leaves unexplained a numerous class of passages to which even its advocates admit that it does not apply. A similar evasion is that suggested by Arnold of Rugby, that the language of these Psalms may be, and is to be, applied by the modern reader to the enemies of his soul's peace. But even were this possible, still it would not explain these fearful words as pronounced by the original utterers. Not a few, therefore, have taken the ground that the language is indefensible; that it sprang from the presence of wicked passion in the hearts of God's ancient servants, who could not rise above the level of the dispensation in which they lived; and that we ought not to be surprised at their occasional lapses into human infirmity. This view is regarded by Dr. Hesse (Bampton Lecture, 1872) as that which is least objectionable. Even Tholuck seems to admit that at times there mingled with the holy fire of the Psalmists the unholy fire of personal irritation. This is wholly inadmissible. These Psalms were not random individual utterances, for which the Bible is no more responsible than it is for the speeches in the Book of Job, but they were from the first destined for use in the sanctuary. God, therefore, must be considered as suggesting and approving the prayers which His Church was to offer in the perpetual service of song. The human authors doubtless expressed their own feelings, but they also expressed what the community of God's people ought to feel, and did feel. On any other view it would be difficult, if not impossible, to maintain the inspiration and authority of the Psalter.

The gist of the matter lies in the question, Do these Psalms contain the malignant expression of ill-will to personal enemies as such, or are they rather the utterance of God's punitive wrath against His obstinate foes? Surely it is not difficult to maintain the latter. The assumption that the Old Testament cherished a vindictive spirit and tolerated resentment for private injuries, is wholly unfounded. In the Pentateuch itself we read, "If thou meet thine enemy's ox or his ass going astray, thou shalt surely bring it back to him" (Exodus xxiii. 4). "Thou shalt not avenge nor bear any grudge against the children of the people, but shall love thy neighbor as thyself" (Leviticus xix. 18). So in Job, "If I rejoice in the destruction of him that hated me, or lifted up myself when evil found him; neither have I suffered my mouth to sin by wishing a curse upon his soul" (xxxi. 29, 30). The prescription of the law (Exodus xxi. 23), "Life for life, eye for eye, tooth for tooth, hand for hand," etc., has been ignorantly quoted as if it laid down the rule for individuals in redressing their own wrongs, whereas it simply states the penalty which the magistrates are to exact from a wrong-doer. Indeed, so far from the Old Testament being at war with the New on this point, we find the Apostle, in dissuading his Roman brethren from taking matters into their own hands, going back to the book of Deuteronomy and quoting its words as a rule, "Dearly beloved, avenge not yourselves, but rather give place unto wrath; for it is written, 'Vengeance is Mine, I will repay,' saith the Lord." And that these inculcations were not fruitless is shown by many examples, and especially that of David. He was a man of intense force of will, and of very strong passions, yet he often exhibited great meekness and forbearance even in trying circumstances. His conduct toward Saul from first to last indicated a spirit anything but malignant and revengeful; and the same is true of his deportment under Shimei's bitter reproaches. Nor can his dying charge to Solomon, respecting Joab and Shimei, be said, if all the circumstances are considered, to be a case of hate projecting itself beyond the grave, but rather of wisdom securing at a future time that satisfaction of justice which could not be attained in the present.  This statement is sustained by his own words.  In Psalm 7th, 4, 5, he invokes wrath upon his head if he has rewarded evil to one that was at peace with him, and affirms on the contrary that he had delivered the man that was without cause his enemy. So in the very Psalm which contains some sore imprecations, the 35th, we find that David refers to personal foes in a very different manner,—

They rewarded me evil for good,
My soul was bereaved.
But as for me, when they were sick, my clothing was sackcloth ;
I afflicted my soul with fasting,
And my prayer returned into my own bosom.
I behaved myself as if it had been my friend, my brother ;
I bowed down heavily as one that mourneth for a mother.

It seems to be evident, then, that when David poured out his awful maledictions, it was not from a mean and base desire to see his personal enemies laid low.  So far as he, himself, was concerned, he could afford to forgive and forget. But his enemies were also enemies of the Lord, and he could rightfully desire and rejoice in their destruction when that dread result was necessary to vindicate God's justice, and demonstrate the reality and power of His government. Thus, in Psalm 58th, the singer, after denouncing unjust and oppressive rulers, and supplicating their rapid and hopeless overthrow, concludes:

The righteous shall rejoice when he seeth the vengeance,
He shall wash his feet in the blood of the wicked.
So that men shall say, Verily there is a reward for the righteous,
Verily there is a God that judgeth in the earth.

It is God's honor that is chiefly concerned, and not the personal feelings of any of His servants. There is, therefore, no more individual resentment in these utterances than there is in the tremendous imprecation of Paul, which, though so simple in its words, contains a full equivalent to all the long and varied wishes for vengeance contained in all the imprecatory Psalms put together. "If any man love not our Lord Jesus Christ, let him be Anathema, Maranatha." Surely in this fearful expression the Apostle was gratifying no private grudge, but only exhibiting his intense and perfect sympathy with the merit and the claims of our adorable Redeemer.

But admitting this, why were these awful curses put into the Liturgy of the Church, and so stereotyped for all coming generations? For good reason. It is true the rule of our conduct is to bless and curse not, to pray for them that despitefully use us; and no part of our Lord's example is more binding upon us than His rebuke to James and John for wishing to call down fire from heaven upon the churlish Samaritans, and His own prayer for His murderers upon the cross. But there is danger lest this meekness and forbearance should be misapplied so as to check or lessen that living conviction of the evil of sin, and of the certainty of God's retributive righteousness, which is essential to true Christian character. The Apostle tells us that the civil magistrate is "a revenger to execute wrath upon him that doeth evil"—not simply to preserve order and to deter by example others from wrong-doing, but in the name of God, whose representative and minister he is, to redress the wrongs of outraged justice. This is seen whenever some foul crime has been committed. Meek and gentle souls who scarcely know what malice is by experience, and who would be quite ready to feed and clothe a personal enemy, will feel a righteous indignation, and long and pray that the criminal may be detected and receive the just reward of his crimes.  Now it is just the same sympathy, not with human government, but the divine, that is expressed in the imprecatory Psalms.  The kingdom of God comes not only by showing mercy to the penitent, but by executing judgment upon the impenitent. Was it not so at the deluge, at the deliverance from Egypt, at the destruction of Jerusalem? We need to have the consuming zeal for God which animated the old Hebrew singers, and then their solemn utterances will take their rightful place as just and true.  They will seem as natural and proper as the opening words of Milton's fine sonnet on the Vaudois,—

> Avenge, O Lord! thy slaughtered saints, whose bones
> Lie scattered on the Alpine mountains cold.

The truth is, these Psalms denounce no more against the wicked than what God actually brings upon them.  They simply utter the burden of the Lord concerning His obdurate foes. Is it impossible that a godly mind may become so much at one with the divine mind in these respects, as justly to pray that the Divine Being would do what it would be certainly righteous in Him to do, and what in His time He assuredly will do? In fact, the argument against these imprecations is really an argument against all retributions, and therefore against the moral government of God, against that throne with whose stability the welfare of the universe is identified. Forbearance toward the desperately wicked is injustice and cruelty to the unoffending, and the feeling which demands justice, instead of being malignant, is really benevolent.

As long as men are at ease, reposing amid the comforts of an established Christian society, and breathing an atmosphere of contentment, peace, and moral order, they fail to hear or understand the outcry of God's suffering children, and have little sympathy with a righteous indignation at wrong-doing. But let storm and tempest come, let diabolical iniquity be wrought, let not only law and justice, but humanity and nature be trodden under foot, and at once there is a startling recoil of the soul. Even the meek and patient fall back upon these inspired utterances, and cry out with fervor:

> O Lord God! to whom vengeance belongeth:
> O God, to whom vengeance belongeth, show Thyself.
> Lift up Thyself, Thou Judge of the earth,
> Render a reward to the proud.

Lord, how long shall the wicked,
How long shall the wicked triumph?—(xciv. 1-3).

An irrepressible instinct of human nature planted by the author of that nature unites with the sentiments nourished by the revelation of God's essential and unalterable righteousness in His word to make men long and pray that the doers of evil may be rooted out of the earth.

A signal illustration of this truth is found in what took place at the time of the East Indian mutiny in 1857, when the news of the fearful atrocities perpetrated not only upon men in arms, but upon women and children, reached Europe and America. The first feeling was one of unspeakable horror; then went up from both sides of the Atlantic a terrible cry for revenge. Persons who had no tie of blood or affection or interest with the sufferers, felt the emotion just as much as the nearest relatives. A prominent American author, Dr. O. W. Holmes, wrote the suggestion that England should take down the map of India, and correct it thus: DELHI, *dele*, and declared that the civilized world would say, Amen. Lord Macaulay (*Life*, II., 367-9) said, "It is painful to be so revengeful as I feel myself. I, who can not bear to see a beast or a bird in pain, could look on without winking while Nana Sahib underwent all the tortures of Ravaillac." Again, "Till this year I did not know what real vindictive hatred meant. With what horror I used to read in Livy how Fulvius put to death the whole Capuan Senate in the Second Punic War! And with what equanimity I could hear that the whole garrison of Delhi and all the rabble of the bazaar had been treated in the same way! Is this wrong? Is not the severity which springs from a great sensibility to human suffering, a better thing than the lenity which springs from indifference to human suffering?" Still more marked was the utterance of the great man who stands at the head of living missionaries of the cross, Dr. Alexander Duff, of Scotland. He said, "I could never fully understand how the so-called imprecatory Psalms could be consistent with the teachings of the New Testament, until the Sepoy rebellion broke out with such terrific fury, and foes sprung up filling the land with violence, shaking the foundations of society and of government; threatening towns and cities with pillage, fire, and sword; murdering the innocent and defenceless; persecuting unoffending Christians with especial malignity; making unresisting missionaries a sacrifice to brutal lust and deadly torture, and thus rolling back the tide of Christian civilization, that iniquity might come in again like a flood, and heathenism with all its horrors and idolatry once more set up its seats in the land—not until then could it be properly realized—felt—that there are times in the outbreaking of human passion and human enmity when the pleadings of mercy are vain, and justice, naked, pitiless justice, must draw the sword in a war of righteous self-defence."

On this view of the case, the Psalms in question are not to be apologized for, nor explained away, nor renounced, but to be justified and commended as an integral part of the word of God, as fulfilling an important and necessary function, as suggesting in a most striking and appropriate way that sympathy with God's government, and that jealousy for God's honor which are the strongest moral powers of the soul. They teach us the fundamental difference between the popular notion of goodness as identical with careless, good-natured indulgence, and the Scriptural doctrine of holiness. God, we are told, hates sin, and He directs us to abhor that which is evil; which indeed seems a logical necessity. For a good man must love that which is good; and how can he love the good without hating its opposite? Hence the two are united in one of the prophetic statements of the moral ground of our Lord's exaltation: "Thou hast loved righteousness and hated iniquity." The truest test of religious character is found in the degree of our sympathy with God in His aversion as well as in His complacency. Indeed, a deep sense of moral evil is essential to a true or saving knowledge of God. Hence the value of those portions of holy writ which stimulate and intensify this conviction. The intelligent reader of these Psalms will never fall a prey to the dreamy sentimentalism which enfeebles so much of the piety of our times, or to the rationalistic subtleties which convert sin into a misfortune, or an accident, or a means of good. He will never exalt mercy at the expense of righteousness, and so turn it into feebleness and incapacity. On the contrary, with a healthy moral sense, and in the spirit of power, of love, and of a sound mind, he will be able to adopt the words which close the 139th Psalm, the crown of the collection, the noble lyric which has attracted the praise of all lands and all scholars:

> Do not I hate them, O Lord, that hate Thee?
> And am not I grieved with those that rise up against Thee?
> I hate them with perfect hatred.
> I count them mine enemies.
> Search me, O God, and know my heart;
> Try me and know my thoughts;
> And see if there be any wicked way in me,
> And lead me in the way everlasting.

To conclude: I have now gone over the leading points of the argument, and stated the teaching of the Psalms upon the nature of God and of man—the two great factors in any scheme of religious thought; upon the contrasted topics of the Messiah and of immortality—one remarkable for the fulness of its treatment, the other for its scantiness and obscurity; and finally, upon the essential features of ethics and worship. In all these respects it has been shown that there is in the Psalter a purity, a correctness, and a spiritual elevation which stamp it as wholly unique among all the literature of its own or any preceding age. And this fact, taken in connection with the character of the book, as not only poetical, but lyrical, and with the circumstances of the region, people, and period in which the collection originated, compel the belief that the sweet singers of Israel sang not only under poetic, but divine inspiration, and that their work is part of an authentic and binding revelation from the living God. This conclusion is greatly strengthened by the subsequent history of the Psalter. For twenty-five centuries its varied contents have maintained a continuous historic life, unbroken by neglect or oblivion—and that, too, among the most widely differing races and countries. They never could be buried under the rubbish of an obsolete literature like the Vedas and the Avestan, nor hid away in the impenetrable darkness of an unknown language like the cuneiform inscriptions. Their very nature gave them an inexhaustible vitality. The ecclesiastical commonwealth, in which they were produced, passed through as many dangers and disasters from without and from within as any of its contemporaries, and at last went down in a tremendous catastrophe. But the Psalms survived, and ever since have been flourishing in immortal youth. The reason is, that they are true. Quite beyond their excellence as poetry, their beauty or finish, or pathos, or lyric fire, they are the living, breathing record of an experience which enters into that which is most characteristic, permanent, and universal in Man, his moral instincts and his spiritual relations to his Maker.

"The deeps of our humanity remain unruffled by the storms of ages which change the surface." It is these deeps to which the Psalms relate. Local and national as they are, they do not treat life after the fashion of any one age or race, but life in its essential and unchangeable elements, and that so thoroughly that every possible state of feeling is represented, and every condition of humanity provided for. As Hooker says, "Let there be any grief or disease incident to the soul of man, any wound or sickness, named, for which there is not in this treasure-house a present comfortable remedy at all times to be found." Each of these divine lyrics is beyond question the true expression of an individual human heart pouring itself out before God, according to its situation at the time; but all observation shows that the writers expressed the joys and sorrows, the struggles and the victories, the fears and the aspirations, not of one man, but of all. Hence the unanimity with which they have been accepted in every age as the inspired directory for worship, both public and private—not simply recognized in form as such, but actually used for every conceivable utterance of prayer and praise. The language of Dean Church is not more expressive than it is true, when, comparing the remains of early heathen religions with the Psalms, he says, "They are like the appearance of the illuminated, but dead surface of the moon, with its burnt-out and extinct volcanoes, contrasted with the abounding light and splendor of the unexhausted sun, still, age after age, the source of life and warmth, and joy to the world, still waking up new energies and developing new wonders." How many in the long track of the ages have had their devotion kindled, their hearts comforted, their affections moulded by this blessed book! To the Jews, alike at the victories under such kings as Jehoshaphat and Hezekiah, or in the bitterness of exile, or in the nascent hopes of the Restoration, the Psalter was the recognized vehicle of thanks or supplication. The Maccabees, in their little-known, but most wondrous struggle, drew their inspiration from the same source. A Psalm brightened the gloom at the last supper of our Lord. And He himself when on the cross expressed His fearful isolation in the words of one Psalm, and in those of another gave up his spirit unto God. When Paul and Silas lay in the prison at Philippi, with feet fast in the stocks, they astonished the other prisoners with the songs of Zion.

These examples were followed by the early Church. "Go where you will," says Jerome, "the ploughman at his plough sings his joyful Hallelujahs, the busy mower regales himself with his Psalms, and the vine-dresser is singing one of the songs of David. These are the solace of the shepherd in his solitude and of the husbandman in his toil." According to Eusebius, the martyrs in the Thebaid employed their latest breath in uttering these divine compositions, just as was done centuries afterward by John Huss and Jerome of Prague, when burning at the stake.* So the army of Gustavus Adolphus, and the Protestants at Courtras, and the Ironsides of Cromwell, and the Covenanters of

---

* In 1663, the town of Kingston, N. Y., was attacked by the Indians, who burned all the houses and carried off a number of prisoners. These were taken far into the wilderness near the Shawangunk river, where preparations were made to torture them to death. The women of the party, to support their drooping spirits, began to sing the songs of Zion. The music attracted the attention of their captors and delayed their proceedings, discovering which, the singers raised Dathenus's version of the 137th Psalm, and poured out its melancholy strains in sight of the spot where the faggots were piled for their torture. Just then deliverance came, the Indians fled, and the songs of mourning were changed to songs of joy—the 137th into the 126th, and the wood intended to consume living bodies was burned to take away the chills of night.—*Edmund Eltinge in Collections of Ulster County Historical Society.* (Kingston, 1860).

Scotland, entered into conflict chanting Psalms, with voices which rose far above the din of battle.

And still in our own day, these old Hebrew lyrics continue to fulfil their high office as a manual of public and private devotion, a stimulus and a comfort amid all the varied experiences of human life. As good Bishop Horne says in a passage of exquisite beauty: "They suit mankind in all situations; grateful as the manna which descended from above and conformed itself to every human palate. The fairest productions of human wit, after a few perusals, like gathered flowers, wither in our hands and lose their fragrancy; but these unfading plants of paradise become, as we are accustomed to them, still more and more beautiful; their bloom appears to be daily heightened; fresh odors are emitted, and new sweets extracted from them. He who hath once tasted their excellencies, will desire to taste them yet again; and he who tastes them oftenest will relish them best." In singular agreement with these statements of the devout English prelate are the utterances of the great German critic, Herder: "Not merely as regards the contents, but also as regards the form, has this use of the

Psalter been a benefit to the spirit and heart of men. As in no lyric poet of Greece or Rome, do we find so much teaching, consolation, and instruction together, so has there scarcely been anywhere so rich a variation of tone in every kind of song as here. For two thousand years have these old Psalms been again and again translated and imitated in a variety of ways, and still so rich, so comprehensive is their manner that they are capable of many a new application. They are flowers which vary according to each season and each soil, and ever abide in the freshness of youth. Precisely because this book contains the simplest lyric tones for the expression of the most manifold feelings, is it a hymn-book for all times." The words of both these eminent men are as true now as when first printed more than a century ago. The Psalms to-day are read by a million times more persons than any other poems in the world, and yet their flavor is not exhausted. Greeks and Orientals, Romanists and Protestants, Prelatists and Puritans, Lutherans and Reformed, men of all shades of doctrine and polity, and of all degrees of culture and progress; the profound theologian and the humble believer, the ripe Christian and the young convert, the man of elegant taste and the freedman who can just spell out the words, alike refresh themselves at these living springs. The mightiest productions of human genius, the Iliad, the Divina Commedia, the dramas of Shakespeare, are to not a few sealed books, but there never yet was in any age, a single devout soul which did not find in these old Psalms the very best expression of its own best experiences. Even Mr. Francis Newman, after abandoning the Gospel for the Absolute Religion, has to go back to David's lyre to find fitting words to express the inward yearning of the human heart toward God. Having quoted Psalm xlii. 1,—

> As the hart panteth after the water-brooks,
> So panteth my soul after thee, O God!
> My soul is athirst for God,
> Yea, even for the living God,—

he adds: "Then the soul understands and knows that God is her God, dwelling with her more closely than any creature can; yea, neither stars nor sea, nor smiling nature hold God so intimately as the bosom of the soul. All nature is ransacked by the Psalmists for metaphors to express this single thought, God is for my soul, and my soul is for God. Father,

Brother, Friend, King, Master, Shepherd, Guide, are common titles. God is their Tower, their Glory, their Rock, their Shield, their Sun, their Star, their Joy, their Portion, their Trust, their Life."

Surely a book thus profound and tender, thus suited to all lands and ages, thus attested by scores of generations, dear to lowly Christians, and yet compelling the suffrage of unbelievers, always tried and yet never found wanting, as eagerly and usefully read to-day in Oregon or Oceanica as it was in the hill country of Judah before the Trojan war; such a book must have a higher than human origin.

# PASSAGES OF SCRIPTURE QUOTED
## OR
# REFERRED TO.

| Reference | Page |
|---|---|
| Exodus, xxi. 23 | 170 |
| " xxiii. 4 | 169 |
| Leviticus, xix. 18 | 169 |
| Deuteronomy, vi. 4 | 40 |
| " xviii. 11 | 134 |
| " xxxii. 35 | 170 |
| Joshua, x. 13 | 86 |
| 2 Samuel, i. 18 | 86, 88 |
| 2 Kings, xix. 15 | 40 |
| Job, xxv. 5 | 52 |
| " xxxi. 29, 30 | 170 |
| Psalm i. | 153 |
| " ii. | 39, 117 |
| " iv. 6 | 94 |
| " vi. | 15, 16, 136 |
| " vii. 4, 5 | 171 |
| " viii. | 75 |
| " xiii. | 16 |
| " xiv. | 78 |
| " xv. | 155 |
| " xvi. | 94, 134 |
| " xvii. | 135 |
| " xviii. | 30, 164 |
| " xix. 12, 13 | 161 |
| " xxii. | 54 |
| " xxix. | 44 |
| " xxx. 9 | 136 |
| " xxxi. | 16 |
| Psalm xxxii. | 15 |
| " xxxiii. 6 | 47 |
| " " 9 | 41 |
| " xxxv. 4-6 | 166 |
| " " 12-14 | 171 |
| " xxxvi. | 15 |
| " xl. 8 | 163 |
| " xliv. | 14 |
| " xlv. | 119 |
| " xlvii. | 99 |
| " xlix. | 135 |
| " l. | 54, 55, 158 |
| " li. 5 | 15, 79 |
| " liii. 1-3 | 78 |
| " lviii. 3 | 79 |
| " " 10, 11 | 172 |
| " lx. | 14 |
| " lxvii. | 103 |
| " lxviii. | 100 |
| " lxix. 24-27 | 166 |
| " lxxi. 22 | 51 |
| " lxxii. | 120 |
| " lxxiii. 24 | 136 |
| " " 25, 26 | 96 |
| " lxxiv. | 14 |
| " lxxvi. 2 | 97 |
| " lxxix. | 14 |
| " lxxxvii. | 101 |

| | | |
|---|---|---|
| Psalm lxxxviii. 10, 11 | 136 | |
| " lxxxix. | 47 | |
| " xc. | 14, 48 | |
| " xciii. | 120 | |
| " xciv | 175 | |
| " xcv. | 102 | |
| " xcvii. | 54 | |
| " c. 3 | 54 | |
| " " 5 | 75 | |
| " " 1–3 | 102 | |
| " cii. | 15, 103 | |
| " " 25–27 | 46 | |
| " ciii. 7 | 97 | |
| " " 8, 9, 11 | 92 | |
| " " 10–17 | 55 | |
| " civ. | 28–30 | |
| " cv. | 68 | |
| " cix. | 167 | |
| " cx. | 39, 122 | |
| " cxi. 9 | 52 | |
| " cxv. 1 | 86 | |
| " " 3 | 47 | |
| " cxix. | 161–163 | |
| " cxxvi. | 184 | |
| Psalm cxxx. | 15, 80 | |
| " " 2 | 180 | |
| " cxxxv. 6 | 42 | |
| " cxxxvi. | 55 | |
| " cxxxvii. | 184 | |
| " " 8, 9 | 167 | |
| " cxxxix. 1–4 | 50 | |
| " " 6 | 51 | |
| " " 7–10 | 49 | |
| " " 17, 18 | 93 | |
| " " 21–24 | 179 | |
| " cxliii. | 15 | |
| " " 2 | 80, 164 | |
| " cxlvii. 19, 20 | 97 | |
| Isaiah, viii. 19 | 134 | |
| " xlv. 6 | 40 | |
| " lx. 1 | 21 | |
| Matthew, vii. 20 | 149 | |
| Acts, xvii. 28 | 74 | |
| Romans, iii. 10 | 78 | |
| " vii. 22 | 162 | |
| " xii. 19 | 170 | |
| 2 Corinthians, xi. 21–31 | 165 | |

# INDEX.

Apologetics, 4, 150.
Aratus, quotation from, 74.
Arnold of Rugby on the Imprecations, 168.
Asaph, his noble Ps., 95, 135.
Asceticism absent from the Psalter, 156.
Athenians, their claim to be autochthons, 74; Moral earnestness, 84.
Augustine's famous saying, 94.
*Avatara*, the Hindu, 128.
Avestan, 3, 62, 87, 92, 128, 181.

Bacon, calls some Pss. "hearse-like," 16.
Books of the Pss., The Five, 13, 14.
Bryant's Thanatopsis, ignores God, 44.

Callimachus, his hymns, 58.
Calvin, on Maccabean Pss., 14; on the 139th, 49.
Church, Dean, on ancient hymns, 83, 182.
Cleanthes, Hymn of, 68, 74.
Clement of Alexandria on Egyptian Idolatry, 132.
Coleridge on Love, 10; on Immortality, 141.

David, retrospect of life, 30–32; Confession of Sin, 79; Conflict with Saul, 165; not vindictive, 170.
Delitzsch on the 29th Ps., 44.
Deutch, E., on the Talmud, 62.
Didactic Pss., 17, 153, 161.

East India Mutiny, 176.
Egypt, not the source of Hebrew Poetry, 24; its idolatry, 106; Doctrine of Immortality, 133, 139, 137.
Eltinge, Edmund, quoted, 184.
Eternity of God, 47.
Ethics of the Psalter, not overstrained, 156; pure, 157; spiritual, 160; joyful, 161.
Eusebius on the Martyrs of the Thebaid, 184.
Ewald, on Maccabean Pss. 15; on Hebrew drama, 21; on lyric poetry, 22; on the 53d Ps., 78; on the 73d, 96.

Fijians, their view of Immortality, 132.
Forgiveness of injuries taught in the Old Testament, 169.
Froude on Ps. cix., 167.

Gibbon, on pure morals of the early Church, 150.
Goethe referred to, 26.
Golden Age, put in the past by heathen, 98; in the future by the Psalmists, 99, 105.
Greek Tragedy, its Nemesis, 84.

Happy Man, The, 153.
Herder, on the Old Testament, 8; on the Pss., 185.
Hesiod, his Theogony, 58.
Hesse, Dr. H., on the Imprecations, 168.
Hindus's Confession of Sin, 81–83.
Holmes, Dr. O. W., quoted, 176.
Holiness of God, 51, 83.
Homeric Hymns, 57, 152.
Horne, Bp., on the Imprecations, 167; on the Pss., 185.
Horsley, Bp., on the Imprecations, 167.
Human heroes, not found in the Psalter, 88, 115.
Humboldt on the 104th Ps., 29.

Ideal Messiah denied, 91.
Immensity of God asserted, 49.

Immortality of the Soul, not *per se* important, 131; known to the Jews, 133; not emphasized, 137; a universal tradition or belief, 141.
Imprecations in the Pss., 166.

Jasher, Book of, its nature, 86-88.
Jebb, Bp., quoted, 20.
Jerome, on use of the Pss., 184.
Justice of God asserted, 53.

Lewis, Prof. Tayler, on the Bible as best defence against error, 6.
Livingstone on Central African beliefs, 133.
Lowth on Parallelism, 19.
Lyrics, Nature of, 9, 10, 152.

Macaulay, Lord, his search for ballads, 23; on the India Mutiny, 176, 177.
Man, not the subject of lyric praise, 28, 86, 115.
Messiah, triumphant, 117; suffering, 123; not found elsewhere in equal purity, 128.
Milton, quotation from Liberty of Unlicensed Printing, 6; from his Sonnet on the Vaudois, 174.
Molière, 58.
Monotheism, characteristic of the Pss., 66; not a question of race, 65.
Morals of the Psalter, pure, 152; rooted in religion, 154, gracious, 156.
Moses, author of the 90th Ps., 13, 14.
Muller, Max, on Vedic Hymns, 60; on Immortality, 131.

Necromancers, among the Jews, 134; modern, 142.
Nemesis of Greek Tragedy, 84.
Newman, Dr. J. H., referred to, 34.
Newman, Prof. Francis, quoted, 187.

Old Testament, foundation of the New, 8, 151; not vindictive, 169.
Omnipresence of God, 49.
Omniscience of God, 50.
Origin of Man, 74.
Ovid, 81.

Palestine, its physical peculiarities, 25.
Pantheism known to the Psalter, 40.
Parallelisms in Hebrew Poetry, 19.
Pascal on man's dignity, 77.
Pessimism, not found in the Psalter, 91.
Penitential Pss., 15.
Poetry of the Psalter, real, 17-21; lyrical, 21-23; Palestinian, 24-26; true, 27.
Pindar, contrast with the Psalter, 86.

Renan on Monotheism, 65.
Robertson of Brighton, his vindication of Wordsworth, 43.

Self-righteousness not justly chargeable to the Psalter, 164.
Soul, its yearning for God, 94, 187.
*Sosiosh*, the Persian, 128.
Spirituality of the Psalter, 11.
Spontaneity of the Pss., 9.
Stanley, Dean, on the Imprecations, 167.

Talmud, 62.
Taylor, Isaac, on Palestine, 25; on mythical heroes, 90.
Tennyson quoted, Charge, etc., 89; Locksley Hall, 104; In Memoriam, 105, 104.
Theology of the Psalter, 39, etc.
Tholuck on the Imprecations, 168.
Truth of all poetry, 27; of the Pss., 28-32.

Unity of God, 39, 66–68.

Varuna's greatness, 61, 62.
Vedas, Age of, 59; Character, 60; fine sayings of, 61; confession of sin, 81; vagueness, 92; earthly, 94.

Whewell on the 8th Ps., 75.
Wordsworth, his pantheistic tendencies, 43.

Zendic Hymns, elevated, 62; Dualistic, 63; their *Sosiosh* post Biblical, 129.

www.ingramcontent.com/pod-product-compliance
Lightning Source LLC
Chambersburg PA
CBHW021732220426
43662CB00008B/816